CRISIS-READY TEAMS

HIGH RELIABILITY AND CRISIS MANAGEMENT
Series Editors: Karlene H. Roberts and Rangaraj Ramanujam

CRISIS-READY TEAMS

Data-Driven Lessons from Aviation,

Nuclear Power, Emergency Medicine,

and Mine Rescue

Mary J. Waller and

Seth A. Kaplan

Stanford Business Books
An Imprint of Stanford University Press
Stanford, California

Stanford University Press
Stanford, California

Special discounts for bulk quantities of Stanford Business Books are available to corporations, professional associations, and other organizations. For details and discount information, contact the special sales department of Stanford University Press by emailing sales@www.sup.org.

Printed in the United States of America on acid-free, archival-quality paper

Library of Congress Cataloging-in-Publication Data
Names: Waller, Mary J., author. | Kaplan, Seth A., author.
Title: Crisis-ready teams : data-driven lessons from aviation, nuclear power, emergency medicine, and mine rescue / Mary J. Waller and Seth A. Kaplan.
Other titles: High reliability and crisis management.
Description: Stanford, California : Stanford Business Books, an imprint of Stanford University Press, 2024. | Series: High reliability and crisis management | Includes index.
Identifiers: LCCN 2023058020 (print) | LCCN 2023058021 (ebook) | ISBN 9781503601444 (cloth) | ISBN 9781503639713 (ebook)
Subjects: LCSH: Crisis management. | Teams in the workplace.
Classification: LCC HD49 .W365 2024 (print) | LCC HD49 (ebook) | DDC 658.4/056—dc23/eng/20240213
LC record available at https://lccn.loc.gov/2023058020
LC ebook record available at https://lccn.loc.gov/2023058021

Cover design: Daniel Benneworth-Gray
Cover art: Unsplash/Shaun Darwood
Typeset by Newgen in 10.5 Garamond pro Regular

Mary
To Birgit, und für unsere große, schöne Familie

Seth
To Aiden, my parents, Jennifer, and Alex for all their support

CONTENTS

PREFACE

As organizations face increasingly complex, turbulent, and unpredictable environments, they will rely more and more on teams, rather than on single individuals, to address crisis situations when they arise. It makes sense to bring together a team of people, pool together members' unique skills, experiences, and ideas, and develop coordinated and informed decisions through their interaction. Crisis situations in organizations are multifaceted and require simultaneous actions, making the idealized image of the lone hero—barking orders and directing action single-handedly—just that: idealized, and appropriate perhaps for Hollywood portrayals, but certainly not for the crisis situations that organizations face and we have studied.

Yes, we have studied teams dealing with crisis situations, and together have spent a combined forty-five years doing it, together with our many esteemed colleagues, co-authors, and graduate students who have played integral and often leading roles in the co-published research we describe and summarize in this book. We are deeply grateful for these collaborations. We have studied aviation flight crews, emergency medical teams, seaport crisis management teams, nuclear power plant control room crews, underground mine rescue teams, military, and many other types of teams as they encountered either highly realistic simulated crisis scenarios during training or real crisis situations. We both have spent hundreds and hundreds of hours analyzing audio and video recordings of team interaction and decision making, noting very specific behaviors within teams, and conducting careful statistical analyses or qualitative studies based on the hidden, underlying patterns of those behaviors. Our coding and analyses have been driven by our knowledge of and training in organizational behavior and industrial/organizational psychology, both of which focus on the study of human behavior in organizations. Yes, we have *studied* teams in organizations dealing with crisis situations.

Importantly, one could say, "Hey, I don't work on (or my students don't or won't be working on) a trauma team or flight crew. The crises that my team faces aren't life-threatening. What can I/we take away from research on these exotic teams?" Good question, and we have a good answer: *a lot.* The fundamental behavioral dynamics of teams apply across teams and across contexts, particularly when team members operate under what *they* perceive and experience to be high levels of threat and stress—two hallmarks of team experience in crisis situations. True, other types of "non-exotic" teams may not face crisis outcomes that involve life and limb, but these teams' outcomes may be *extremely* significant to them, their departments, their organizations, and their families, and the stress and threats these teams experience may be at the same levels—or even higher—than those of, say, a highly experienced trauma team. The advantage to collecting data from teams such as trauma teams, flight crews, nuclear power plant crews, and other teams from so-called "high reliability organizations" (organizations that operate in high-risk contexts) is that these teams undergo extremely challenging training in highly realistic simulated scenarios that make it possible for us to observe and study their behavior. As most of our research findings from these team observations have been published in academic journals and are not exactly written to be "accessible" (that is, they are filled with academic jargon and references), one central goal of this book is to summarize and synthesize this research for teams, team members, team leaders, and instructors/trainers for organizations that are not in the "high reliability" or academic worlds. We are intimately familiar with this research, and we believe it can make a positive difference if transferred to a different format and put in the hands of the right people and right teams. Thus, our goal is to provide a usable book on teams and crises that is based on this specific empirical evidence, rather than a compendium or encyclopedia summarizing and citing a broad cross section of literature on team dynamics or crisis management.

Getting this research in a usable form to the right people is important because the research has identified striking, nonobvious factors that allow some teams to experience consistently better crisis situation outcomes than other teams. In fact, teams missing these factors perform at levels well below their counterparts. Yet in many of these studies, when we asked the more successful teams what they believed led to their effectiveness, they produced a lot of good guesses but never once identified the entire complement of behaviors that we found actually set them apart from their peers. *Not once.* However, when we shared our final research results with teams and their trainers, these professionals confirmed the accuracy of the work, often with "aha" moments as the results directly mapped onto feelings or intuitions they had experienced but had never quite completely articulated.

What meaning can we draw from this? That crises are complex and chaotic situations, and it is incredibly difficult to see what behaviors are emerging in a team while one is also trying to figure out what is happening and perform a job. This is especially true during such critical situations; team members must maintain their awareness of what is unfolding, perform complex tasks, adapt to unexpected changes, and coordinate with each other. Adding the simultaneous diagnosis of team dynamics to this list may be beyond the capabilities of most team members. As researchers of teams dealing with crises, however, we use a variety of behavioral observation and statistical techniques to dig beneath the fleeting visible surface of team behavior, and offer an empirical, data-driven, evidence-based view of dynamics in these teams. In contrast to many other books available on the topic of teams facing crises, this book is not based on our personal experiences as crisis team members; it is also not based on one case study of a particular team facing a particular crisis, *nor* is it based simply on our hunches or opinions. The work presented in this book is based on peer-reviewed, published empirical research that we and our research partners and colleagues have together created. As the book unfolds, the reader will see that this evidence, drawn from published research on a variety of types of teams, builds a compelling case for attention to three central areas of behavior.

BOOK CONTENTS

After an introductory Chapter 1 focused on the intersection of teams and the crises they encounter in organizations, we begin with the three central areas of behavior in order of increasing complexity, starting with Part I and the topic "Setting the Tone." Most of us have heard for years that first impressions matter, but that axiom is generally applied to situations such as job interviews and dating. Current research, however, underscores how the initial moments of a team's interactions can set the stage for the team's later performance during a crisis situation—for those moments when the situation reaches its apex in terms of tension and criticality. Depending on *how* those first few interactions in the team unfold, a team can embark on a path that will either help or hinder its performance just when it needs every advantage it can get. To illustrate setting the tone, we describe research carried out with trauma teams, aviation flight crews, commercial seaport crisis teams, and MBA student teams.

The second area of behavior we turn to in Part II is "Adapting on the Fly." Crises are by their very nature emergent, dynamic situations, and successful teams typically do not simply go into a crisis situation with a plan or a playbook; they continually gather information and adapt to an unfolding crisis in real time. However, the research indicates that high-performing teams engage in *specific* adaptive behaviors in ways that differ significantly from other teams, and they do so consistently and in nonobvious ways. In this section, we use research from aviation flight crews, nuclear power plant crews, and a military team on 9/11 to illustrate these key adaptive behaviors.

In Part III, we focus on "Finding the Balance" as the third behavioral area covered within the context of an unfolding crisis; it is also the most complex of the three, because it involves something we refer to as *tensions*. Tensions require teams to achieve and maintain a balance between two competing forces, and doing so during a crisis situation necessitates a high level of awareness and discipline in a team. In the research we describe, we identify *three* key tensions that can spell the difference between low- and high-performance outcomes for teams facing critical situations. We use research from nuclear power plant crews, aviation flight crews, and underground mine rescue teams as examples of how the appropriate management of these tensions can lead to better team outcomes during critical events.

In these three sections, each focused on an overarching behavior, we've also included ideas for applying the concepts covered to a specific (i.e., one's own) team situation—either to augment an existing action plan for a team, or to create an entirely new one.

The book concludes with Part IV and a focus on "Helping Teams Become Crisis-Ready," covering issues that may increase a team's *ability* to engage in the behaviors associated with Setting the Tone, Adapting on the Fly, and Finding the Balance in the first place. These issues involve "Designing High-Performing Teams for Crises" (Chapter 12), "Training High-Performing Teams for Crises" (Chapter 13), "Enhancing Team Resilience for Crises" (Chapter 14), and awareness of "The Ethics of Crisis Preparation" (Chapter 15). In this final section of the book, we identify some of the possible antecedent factors that lead teams to engage in the behaviors associated with higher performance during critical situations, and then examine how teams could be better prepared for success. We also zoom out and provide a broad view of the significant implications for the people who work in organizations, the people they go home to, and the communities that surround our organizations when our organizations are crisis-prepared—and when they are not.

Again, the overarching goal we have for this book is to put solid, research-based knowledge about crisis-related team dynamics into the hands of people who can really use it: team members and team leaders across different fields, sectors, and industries. The book is particularly appropriate for those who have worked on teams facing critical events and who are poised to lead such teams themselves; rather than have them rely only on practical experience to gain necessary insights, we hope to give these folks a head start concerning the key team behaviors to notice and guide. At the same time, we believe that seasoned team members and leaders will also find value in developing deeper understanding and nuance regarding why certain behaviors are occurring (or are missing) in their teams, and will benefit significantly from what we offer here. We believe this book is also appropriate for use in MBA or executive education instruction on crisis management and leadership.

As we mentioned, this book represents many years of research effort, as well as the support of many additional individuals, including our families, colleagues, graduate students, and staff—particularly Juliet Romero, who helped us tremendously with formatting our manuscript for publication. Thanks to you all for your contributions and encouragement.

Alongside our many talented research colleagues, we have spent years studying teams of real pilots, real nuclear power plant experts, real trauma nurses and physicians, real mine rescuers, and many other professionals as they successfully and unsuccessfully navigated critical situations, and we are deeply grateful for everything these teams and their organizations graciously offered us in terms of access, time, and expertise. Our academic careers benefited from their generosity and openness. We are also very grateful to the institutions that have supported many of our research projects, including the U.S. Federal Aviation Administration, the U.S. Nuclear Regulatory Commission, Ontario Mine Rescue, and the Social Science and Humanities Research Council of Canada.

Unfortunately, much of the knowledge our research teams have generated is hiding in academic journals. Now it is time for us to return the favor to the teams we have studied, and to help share that knowledge more broadly—at a time in the world when teams facing crises might especially benefit from it.

Mary J. ("Mara") Waller, PhD
Seth A. Kaplan, PhD

CRISIS-READY TEAMS

TEAMS AND CRISES

What Is a Crisis? How Do Teams React to Them?

CHAPTER I

HOW TEAMS RESPOND TO RARE, CATASTROPHIC EVENTS: AN OVERVIEW

In 2018, on a normal everyday Southwest Airlines flight from New York to Dallas, an airline with a stellar safety record experienced a catastrophic mechanical failure.

Fragments from a broken engine cowl damaged the fuselage, causing the aircraft to depressurize. One passenger was pulled partially out of the aircraft by the depressurization, and was pulled back into the aircraft by quick-acting fellow passengers. Sadly, that passenger sustained fatal injuries, and several other passengers sustained minor injuries from the event. The aircraft itself was severely damaged, and has never been returned to service as of this writing.[1]

While the flight crew has been commended for its quick action in bringing the severely disabled aircraft to a safe landing in Philadelphia, the Southwest executives and its trained crisis team also deserve credit. With processes in the organization continuously monitoring and combating misinformation on social media, the CEO quickly delivered a forty-second video apology, followed up with numerous fact-filled updates. Simultaneously, Southwest sent a plane loaded with crisis response-trained employees to Philadelphia as its "go-team." Another team flew to the deceased victim's family to help them with travel arrangements.

The organization implements recurrent training for all of its crisis response teams in order to integrate lessons learned. As summarized by the Director of Crisis Response, the firm's stance in such crises is clear: "There's no formula except compassion."[2]

* * *

And there is no substitute for preparation. How many times have we heard those words? But do all organizations need the level of preparedness of an airline? Don't we expect an airline—a so-called "high reliability" organization that operates with complex systems functioning with precision—to be more prepared than others? The problem is that this particular crisis really had little to do with Southwest's ability to precisely manage its own systems. Instead, the problem arose, ostensibly, from the manufacturing of the engine itself—something well outside the control of Southwest. Even for a high-reliability organization like an airline, there are some crises that just can't be precisely prepared for or predicted.

Whether your team is managing a corporate retreat or an aircraft, bad things happen, and they can quickly devolve into crises. Because organizations' external environments have become so incredibly complex, turbulent, and unpredictable, the critical situations they encounter are likewise complex, turbulent, and unpredictable. Consequently, organizations have learned over the past few decades that during a crisis, they cannot only rely on the leader or archetypal hero—featured in countless myths and Hollywood stories—to single-handedly know everything and swoop in to save the day.[3] This *includes* the CEO. Rather, most organizations have found that they need *teams* of individuals that can quickly pool members' unique views and expertise to manage unexpected, complex, critical events. The result: Today, there are more organizations facing more crises and using more *teams* to deal with them.

CRISIS EVENTS

But what *is* a crisis event, exactly, as opposed to other important challenges in organizations, and why is the distinction important? Many scholars have given this significant thought, since people tend to react very differently during crisis events as opposed to other important but non-crisis events. Although several good definitions of crisis exist, our favorite is this comprehensive one from Christine Pearson and Judith Clair:

> *An organizational crisis is a **low-probability, high-impact** situation that is perceived by critical stakeholders to **threaten the viability** of the organization and that is subjectively experienced by these individuals as personally and socially **threatening**. . . . **Ambiguity** of cause, effect, and means of resolution of the organizational crisis will lead to **disillusionment or loss** of psychic and shared meaning, as well as to the **shattering of commonly held beliefs** and values and individuals' basic assumptions. During the crisis, decision making is pressed by **perceived time constraints** and colored by cognitive limitations. (**emphasis** added)[4]*

Pearson and Clair emphasize six fundamental points here. First, crisis events stand out from other important events in organizations based on their rarity and unexpectedness. These are events that take us by surprise, and even though we might have prepared for their eventuality, we can't predict if and certainly not when they might occur.

Second, these are events that have the potential to do significant damage, either financially or in other longer-term ways—for instance, in terms of reputational damage. For example, several years ago, a couple of workers at a Domino's pizza franchise thought it would be great fun to post a video of themselves on social media as they pretended to put all sorts of disgusting things on customers' food orders. The reputational fallout for Domino's was near-immediate thanks to the viral vortex of social media; the two employees ended up with felony charges, and customers' perception of Domino's quality went from positive to negative virtually overnight.[5] Damaging crisis events such as this are threatening both to the organization and to the teams and people in them faced with handling the fallout. This is an important point, because people can react in unpredictable ways to situations they perceive as personally threatening.

Third, in the midst of this event that surprises us and threatens us, we are surrounded by ambiguity; we don't have a clear picture of why the crisis happened, how it is going to affect us, or how to resolve it. Without clarity, some of us freeze, unable to move forward and make decisions with so little to go on; others wait too long, wasting precious time hoping that more information and clarity will arrive.

Fourth, our basic assumptions about how things are supposed to work no longer function, at least not as they normally do. A crisis may render many normal operating procedures, worksheets, checklists, and training manuals obsolete. For example, consider all the normal, taken-for-granted work procedures made instantly obsolete during the early stages of the COVID-19 pandemic. When a crisis event turns basic assumptions upside down, this places people within what Karl Weick refers to as a "cosmology episode":

A cosmology episode happens when people suddenly feel that the universe is no longer a rational, orderly system. What makes such an episode so shattering is that people suffer from the event and, at the same time, lose the means to recover from it. In this sense, a cosmology episode is the opposite of a déjà vu experience. In moments of déjà vu, everything suddenly feels familiar, recognizable. By contrast, in a cosmology episode, everything seems strange. A person feels like he has never been here before, has no idea of where he is, and has no idea who can help him. An inevitable state of panic ensues, and the individual becomes more and more anxious until he finds it almost impossible to make sense of what is happening to him.[6]

Added to the fog of a potential cosmology episode, we have Pearson and Clair's fifth point: It is clear that the situation must be resolved *immediately*.

Imagine feeling threatened by not understanding why an event is happening, what its implications are, or how you will be affected, then finding that your skills, rules, routines, and procedures are useless, and knowing that something must be done immediately. In these situations, people *tend* to: make snap judgments, lose our tempers, have tunnel vision, shut down, grasp at straws, flail around—in short, do things they would not normally do, as they experience the cognitive limitations that Pearson and Clair note in their sixth point. We are *human*, and so are the teams that are called upon to coordinate and deal with the crisis quickly and effectively.

It is thus not surprising to see or participate on teams that perform poorly in crisis situations. But if teams are composed of humans, and humans have general tendencies to freeze up, close down, panic, and so forth under threatening crisis situations, why is it that some teams actually *excel* during crises? Take, for example, the NEADS (Northeast Air Defense Sector—now known as the Eastern Air Defense Sector) team on 9/11. This military team, then located in a bunker in Upstate New York, was trained and charged with the responsibility of protecting U.S. airspace from incoming threats. On September 11, 2001, the team, led by Major Kevin Nasypany, was expecting to be involved in a training exercise when it learned of a possible hijacking. Scrambling to establish communication links with the Federal Aviation Administration (FAA), military fighter jets, and other sources, the team collected new information and learned of more possible hijackings, crashes, and threats, flexibly updating its understanding of the situation from training exercise to protocol hijacking to coordinated terrorist attack over an amazingly short period of time.[7] Had NEADS ever actually trained to handle exactly this type of event? Of course not—no one had envisioned such an attack taking place. Why was the NEADS team so effective during the crisis it faced? We will consider this question in more depth particularly for NEADS later, in Chapter 7.

One could think that if their team doesn't face life-threatening crises, with no team members' lives at stake, and no team decisions that have life-or-death outcomes, then all this does not apply to them. We would emphatically reject this notion. The experiences of fear and threat and all the crisis elements identified by Pearson and Clair are also present during countless non-life-threatening organizational crises. The same basic reactions, while certainly not as intense, could be present when team members fear severe retribution, job loss, public humiliation, or even losing a powerful, important client during a crisis situation.

CRISIS TYPES

While there are many organizing frameworks for organizational crises, our favorite is from Otto Lerbinger, who categorizes possible organizational crises in seven ways.[8] The examples for Confrontation, Malevolence, Mismanagement, and Skewed Management Values—four crisis types that subsume a large number of crises in organizations today—do not necessarily involve life-threatening situations for victims or team members.

TABLE I.   Examples of Some Crisis Types

Type	Description	Possible Examples
Confrontation	Confrontation, protest, boycott, and/or picket carried out by opposing group	1995—Greenpeace vs. Shell re: Brent Spar confrontation
Malevolence	Extreme or criminal actions taken to damage or obtain gain from an organization	2021—JBS hack and ransomware attack
Mismanagement	Violation or ignorance of basic management principles (e.g., negligence, incompetence, inadequate control, and oversight)	2017—United Airlines removal of paid passenger due to flight overbooking
Skewed Management Values	Placing short-term economic gain over broader social values and standards (e.g., profits over people)	2007—Mattel toy recall

Now imagine the teams inside these organizations addressing some of these crises. For example, the team handling the rough removal of a seated passenger due, purportedly, to an airline's own overbooking system made some interesting decisions—none of them life-threatening, to our knowledge, but certainly highly consequential to the airline's reputation and litigation.

CRISIS TEAMS

In addition to categorizing crisis types, we can also characterize crisis teams in organizations based on their characteristics. This is a useful exercise; what is called a "crisis team" in one organization may differ significantly from the type of team that is called upon to deal with crisis situations in a similar organization. One source of confusion in our conversations about teams and crises, in our opinion, emanates from the "apples to oranges" comparison of the wide variety of teams that are called upon to handle crises.

First, there is the type of team that is a designated "crisis team" in its organization. Here, members train regularly as a team and are prepared for a range of crises. The standing crisis team at Southwest Airlines that jumped into action in our vignette that opened this chapter is a good example of a crisis team. In fact, because we believe the label "crisis team" should only be applied to these types of teams—teams that receive recurrent training and that are designated to address crisis situations—we only use the label "crisis team" in this book to refer to these types of teams.

Sometimes, a crisis team is a team with one main purpose: to respond to crisis events. This would include teams such as firefighting teams—teams that have responding to critical situations as their central function. In other instances, crisis teams perform routine, often highly complex everyday activities during the majority of their workday, but are *also* trained and responsible for handling sudden crises. Nuclear power plant control room crews and many cybersecurity teams are examples here. Large organizations' top management teams, like the executive team at Southwest that undergoes recurrent crisis training, also often fit this description.

You can contrast the first type of team (like firefighters) as *single-purpose* crisis teams, and the second type (like cybersecurity teams) as *dual-purpose* crisis teams. The first type has one job: responding to a crisis, while the second type has dual jobs: routine tasks that they perform most of the time, *and* responding to unlikely crisis events.[9] One might also distinguish dual-purpose teams in which membership is stable from those in which membership is temporary. An apt example here is the difference between nuclear power plant crews and commercial flight crews. Most of the nuclear power plant crews we studied in the United States had been working together as teams for a number of years. In contrast, due to the complex scheduling algorithms used by airlines for (often) thousands of pilots flying and based in different geographic areas, pilots rarely fly with the same pilots as a flight crew for more than a few legs (segments) of flight.

Finally, there are crisis teams that emerge "on the spot" solely to combat the crisis and disband once the crisis has abated. Here, team membership usually reflects some combination of expertise and availability. A prominent example of this model is Code Blue teams in hospitals. In most cases, the Code Blue team consists of the physicians and nurses who happen to be available and close by when the patient "codes" and needs immediate resuscitation. The team is based on relevant roles and expertise but also on availability and proximity.

Of course, there are other types of teams that fall between these types. However, we suggest this typology is still a useful categorization in thinking about the types of teams that respond to crises.

To summarize, organizational environments have never been more complex, uncertain, unforgiving, and absolutely ripe for crises. These crises befall organizations in myriad configurations, and organizations have responded by creating teams with various characteristics to address them. However, as

TABLE 2.   Typology of Crisis Teams

	Definition and Examples
Single-Purpose Crisis Teams	Teams that exist only to respond to crises; firefighting teams, some police and military teams
Dual-Purpose Crisis Teams with Stable Membership	Stable teams that work together mostly on routine-but-complex tasks, and train together to address crises when they occur; nuclear power plant control room crews, *some* top management teams
Dual-Purpose Crisis Teams with Variable Membership	Temporary teams that work together mostly on routine-but-complex tasks, and train members to address crises in variable teams when they occur; commercial flight crews, hospital trauma teams
Ad-Hoc Crisis Teams	Temporary teams that form on the spot only to address a crisis, with members trained to do so; hospital Code Blue teams

humans—and, thus, as human teams—we have some hardwired responses to the types of threats we are likely to perceive during crisis situations; these responses are not always advantageous, and they can be difficult to short-circuit.

So why is it that some teams are more effective than others—holding type of crisis and type of team constant—at dealing with crisis events? The teams may all be composed of very similar-seeming individuals with comparable education and experience. But when a nasty, unexpected crisis event occurs, a team that deals with a crisis effectively looks like a ballet, or better yet, like a well-oiled machine, with all the parts synchronized, and people anticipating each other's moves and needs. A team that is less effective looks awkward and stilted during a crisis, with fits and starts, missed opportunities and misunderstandings. But these are only the surface cues that we can see immediately and easily. What are the underlying *behavioral patterns* that separate the effective teams from the ineffective ones during crises? And what do we mean by behavioral patterns?

BEHAVIORAL PATTERNS IN TEAMS

As human beings, we are motivated to reduce uncertainty. We cannot avoid this tendency. It was probably to our ancestors' advantage millennia ago to be safe rather than sorry and stick to the routine when foraging and deciding whether or not to try that unusual-looking mushroom. Although we try to control our biases, we have a preference for interacting in all sorts of different social settings with people we believe are similar to us. Why? We believe we can anticipate them—what they will say, how they will say it, what they will find acceptable or unacceptable. In other words, the *uncertainty* of the social interaction is decreased significantly if we're interacting with people who are like us on some level.

Given our penchant for reducing uncertainty, it is no wonder that we are also really good at falling into behavioral patterns—so good, in fact, we don't even realize it is happening. Rather than go through the uncertainty of doing things differently every day, we easily fall into patterns of behaviors (routines or habits) that we use again and again. Have you ever caught yourself walking (or driving) to work only to realize you were halfway there and didn't remember anything about the first half of your trip? You were deep in thought about what your day was going to be like, or what happened the night before, and your behavioral pattern that got you to work every day simply became automatic. The first couple of times you walked or drove to work, you had to think about it, but after that, it became part of your pattern repertoire.

Just as individuals fall into behavioral patterns, so too do teams. And similar to individuals, teams are unaware these patterns are emerging. Consider this example. You are meeting with a new task force this week in a face-to-face setting—seven people in a conference room around a long oval table. There are eight chairs. Everyone is on time and takes a seat. The team agrees to weekly meetings in the same room for the next four weeks. The next week, folks arrive one or two minutes before meeting time. Where do they sit? Five sit exactly where they did during the first meeting; two sit elsewhere. The following week, team members arrive again a few minutes before meeting time. Where do they sit? Correct—exactly where they did for the second meeting. Chances are pretty good that team members will stick to this arrangement now, without a word being said. Why? It decreases uncertainty—everyone knows where their place is and who they will sit next to. What could be more comfortable? And it all emerges quickly and automatically.

Other behavioral patterns in teams emerge even more quickly. Within the first few minutes of talking, the team members of this task force would experience who among them was talkative, who seemed quiet, who was humorous, and who was serious. They would experience if one person seemed ready to take charge or if the team was content for leadership to emerge or be shared. They would experience "communication balance" or a lack of it—that is, if their communication was balanced across all team members with everyone talking in relatively equal proportion, or if one or two team members were dominating the conversation. They would experience if some people were interrupted or ignored more than others, or if their ideas were appropriated by others. All of these experiences would be composed of identifiable behaviors (like asking a question, giving a command, sharing information, and so on) arranged in the same repeatable patterns. And once these patterns emerge in the team, they tend to stay—just like our own individual behavioral patterns and habits.

The team members would experience all of these behavioral patterns, but very likely not be able to tell you about them. They would be much more likely to report that the team seemed productive or good or nice or comfortable, or not. The fact is that humans are *terrible* at recognizing behavioral patterns as they are unfolding.[10] We are much too busy listening to the content of what is being said and formulating our response, or thinking about what we can add to the decision being made. And imagine trying to recognize behavioral patterns in a team during an unfolding crisis, when our stress levels are sky-high and our cognitive and emotional resources are taxed to their limits—well, it would be virtually impossible. But these behavioral patterns matter to team effectiveness, and matter deeply. They emerge in teams and arrange members' coordination and communication efforts over time, spelling the difference in many crisis settings between success and failure. But how, exactly? What exactly do effective and ineffective teams *do* differently during crises? If we could answer these questions, we might have a chance to improve the effectiveness of *most* teams facing crisis situations.

AN EVIDENCE-BASED APPROACH

Considering the proliferation of crisis events and the teams facing them, answering the above question has become something of a holy grail for many people—academics, authors, management consultants, team trainers, and others. A quick perusal of a retailer such as Amazon yields thousands of book titles for "crisis management." Which approach is most appropriate?

First, many of the titles adopt what we refer to as a "story" approach and are based on one person's experience on one team—for instance, how a team at first faltered, then pulled together and scaled a mountain in treacherous conditions, or how a team fell apart and descended into distrustful infighting during a political crisis. While these accounts are informative and sometimes quite riveting, they may be unique, idiosyncratic stories that might not provide enough specific information about team-level behaviors for another team to apply in the crisis situations it encounters.

Second, other purveyors of crisis management wisdom offer approaches that we refer to as "lessons from" approaches. These titles, like the ones described above, tell a story about a particular team or perhaps a group of teams, and suggest that a team facing a crisis situation would be in much better shape if it would simply act like that particular *type* of team—usually a specialized, highly trained military or paramilitary team, such as a SWAT team. The book goes on to provide special hard-to-acquire lessons from that type of team, based on the author's personal experience. If you have ever admired someone and tried to imitate them without really understanding how they were able to do what they did, and your efforts seemed inauthentic, wobbly, and awkward, just imagine how that works for a team trying to act like something it is not, without deeply understanding the behaviors it is imitating, and all during a crisis situation.

A third approach authors use in offering their solutions to team effectiveness during crises is the "secret sauce" approach. These titles usually involve authors recounting their experiences as team leaders in various crisis situations, often in memoir format; the books generally culminate with advice on how teams should handle crisis situations, as based on the unique personal experience of the author. Of course, the advice provided is framed by authors' experiences as accompanied by their potential biases and perceptions of the situations recounted, as is possible in any memoir. This is certainly not to lessen authors' achievements, but instead to remind us that even achievement-based wisdom is idiosyncratic and might not be the best fit for a wide variety of particular teams facing crisis situations.

While all three of the above approaches—"story," "lessons from," and "secret sauce"—offer information about teams facing crisis situations, they often lack two important qualities. First, they frequently do not involve empirical research, and thus are often light in scientific rigor. What do we mean by that, and why is it so important? The National Institutes of Health (NIH) defines scientific rigor this way:

Scientific rigor is the strict application of the scientific method to ensure unbiased and well-controlled experimental design, methodology, analysis, interpretation and reporting of results.[11]

Keeping in mind that *no* method of inquiry is infallible, when research studies are carried out by following the principles of the scientific method (whether the designs are "experiments" or use another form of data collection, such as behavioral observation studies), we may feel more confident in putting our trust in and acting upon the studies' conclusions. Following the scientific method means that the studies are designed to minimize many sources of bias; additionally, studies that go through the "double-blind" review process required by most reputable academic journals are put through the ringer by expert reviewers before they can be published. These reviewers, who don't know the identity of the authors (and the authors don't know who the reviewers are—thus the "double-blind" label) may require authors to make improvements to their work before it is published, or may opt to reject the work for publication altogether. In fact, many top academic journals that publish research on teams facing crisis situations (for instance, *Journal of Applied Psychology, Journal of Organizational Behavior, Academy of Management Journal*, and others) routinely reject at least 80 to 90 percent of the research manuscripts they receive. All of this combines to allow some trust in conclusions drawn from rigorous studies published in top academic journals. Think of it as one quality seal of approval. In contrast, it seems to us that many of the titles in the three categories of books described above contain accounts that are informative and extremely interesting, but may not be based on rigorous published research studies that allow conclusions to be applied to very many situations.

The second quality typically found wanting in these types of books about teams facing crises is a little more opaque. In the "story," "lessons from," and "secret sauce" approaches, things often unfold with the story first explaining what happened, followed by a list of general takeaways that the author suggests we draw from the story. A couple of things are often missing here.

First, what specific team behaviors lead to *both* high and low performance for the crisis situation in question? In other words, if the team in the story succeeded, what would an unsuccessful team's behavior have looked like, so we know what to avoid? How do we know that the successful team wasn't just lucky? Similarly, if the team in the story was unsuccessful, what would a successful team's behavior have looked like—a mirror image of the unsuccessful team? How do we know if simply avoiding the unsuccessful team's behavior is all we need to do in order to be successful?

The second thing typically missing from these books is the inclusion of *detailed* characteristics of team behaviors in crisis situations. It is not enough to say, for example, that a successful team "communicated" well; exactly *how* did it communicate, and *when*? What were its *patterns* of communication over time, and during what *parts* of the crisis event? Stories about teams facing crisis situations are often rich accounts and interesting to read, but they also often give us little to go on in the way of specific behaviors that set high-performing teams apart. They either do not include the level of behavioral precision we need in order to transfer the information to our own teams, or the stories don't include direct comparisons of both high- and low-performing teams in the same situation, or both.

This brings us to the approach we have adopted for this book. Rather than recount our experiences with one team (the "story" approach), suggest you should adopt the methods of one *type* of team (the "lessons from" approach), or offer a memoir-type chronological recounting of what we have personally

TABLE 3.   Typical Approaches for Books on Teams Facing Crises

Approach	Advantages	Disadvantages
Story	Interesting to read Often first-person accounts with extra information about the situation	Not enough detailed behavioral information to apply to other teams Idiosyncratic view; typically not rigorous research
Lessons From	Interesting to read Hard-to-get information from specialized teams	Not enough detailed behavioral information to apply to other teams Idiosyncratic view; typically not rigorous research
Secret Sauce	Interesting to read Often recount several episodes over multiple situations	Not enough detailed behavioral information to apply to other teams Idiosyncratic view; typically not rigorous research
Evidence-based research	Rigorous research based on vetted methods Often includes detailed behavioral information that could be used with other teams	Difficult to read if in academic journals Practical application of findings often unclear Often difficult to find or expensive to access

learned over the past almost-three decades of work (the "secret sauce" approach), we have chosen an *evidence-based approach* for this book. The three sections of the book that follow are based on the results of ten research studies, most involving numerous teams, that we have conducted with our colleagues around the world. At this writing, eight of the ten studies have been published in rigorous academic journals; one study is currently under review at a journal and has been presented at a peer-reviewed academic conference; and the other study is a published book chapter in an academic book.

All of these rigorous studies are based on data collected from teams facing crisis situations; nine of the ten studies involve the analysis and comparison of specific behaviors between low- and high-performing teams. We have organized the results from the studies into three book sections: Setting the Tone, Adapting on the Fly, and Finding the Balance. These topics, based on the research we will describe, represent the most critical points during crises where the behaviors of low- and high-performing teams diverge. In each section, we explain what the general situation is—for example, the beginning moments of teams working together during critical situations in our section on setting the tone—and then we explain in detail how the high-performing teams' behaviors differed from other teams in the research. We have summarized the research and we explain it clearly, including the citations to the original research articles if you want even more detail. We tell you exactly how you can go about leveraging the research results in your own situation with your own team: At the end of each individual chapter, we include a list of Practical Takeaways to help you do just that. Additionally, we include a summarizing Checklist at the end of each section.

We have three more points to add here about this book. First, throughout all these evidence-based chapters, you will find the notion of *adaptation* is key. The behaviors we have pinpointed with empirical research allow teams to continuously adapt to unexpected crisis situations. Exceptional teams do not adapt only once when a crisis hits and then power on; they continuously check in, updating their understanding of a morphing, dynamic situation. This allows a team to stay ahead of the crisis curve, rather than just running in place or, worse yet, running behind the curve, trying to catch up with the crisis that has left them behind.

Second, our focus is on understanding team performance within organizations during *event-based crises*. We have focused our efforts on identifying what specific behaviors a team should use in response to a specific crisis event or scenario that has occurred in a specific organizational setting. An example might be studying what behaviors lead to better performance among trauma teams facing a patient who presents them with a specific set of unexpected critical problems combined with an equipment failure. This is in contrast to two other similar but distinctly different areas of inquiry. One focuses on organizations *in crisis*. This area of research investigates the trajectory of organizational decline, following organizations as they experience (or help cause) crisis after crisis over a long period of time, and may include the actions of teams during the decline. The other area of inquiry focuses on *disaster management*. This area of research, which has grown significantly over the last few decades, focuses on the coordination of private and public teams, organizations, and resources during wide-scale crises such as floods, hurricanes, and pandemics that affect many organizations simultaneously.

Finally, a word about what we do *not* cover in this book. First, although we do provide many practical implications drawn from our research for team leaders and members, we do not focus extensively on leaders, leadership styles, or leadership development in our research. Teams facing crisis situations can have many types of leadership arrangements: formal leaders, informal leaders, shared leadership, rotating leadership, emergent leadership, and various permutations of these arrangements. We focus on identifying and explaining what team-level behaviors separate high-performing teams from other teams during crisis situations, regardless of their leadership structure. Why? Even if a team has a formal leader, this does not necessarily mean that shared leadership did not emerge during a crisis event. Likewise, even if a team supposedly has a shared leadership structure, this does not mean that someone did not assume a clear leader role when a crisis emerged. Thus, although leadership is certainly a fascinating topic, our focus here is on identifying and understanding what those key, impactful team behaviors are during crisis situations, and when they occur.

And second, our focus is on those key team behaviors during the acute, "hot" stage of dealing with a crisis situation; as a result, and as you will see below, although we will certainly emphasize the importance of crisis preparation and training, we will not be describing in detail all the steps involved in topics like long-range business continuity planning, succession planning, or other subjects that, while certainly important, reach farther out into the future than our temporal research lens.

PREPARING TEAMS FOR CRISES

Of course, knowing which behaviors distinguish high-performing teams from other teams in a crisis situation is one thing; understanding why only *some* teams engage in those behaviors in the first place is something entirely different. For example, as we noted at the beginning of this chapter, Southwest Airlines had a trained crisis team ready to respond to the situation it faced; in fact, on that day, the company's executive team was assembled to go through its own recurrent crisis management training. Adaptive crisis management—the approach typically adopted by crisis-prepared organizations—revolves around the realization that organizations and the teams in them will *never* be able to perfectly predict the timing and nature of the next crisis, but they can practice and hone the *capabilities* that will allow them to adapt to and better manage the infinite variety of crisis events possible. Crisis-prepared organizations also tend to do a much better job setting their teams up for success in *three specific ways*: team member selection, team training, and team resilience. In Chapters 12, 13, and 14 of this book, we will take a close look at how organizations can manage these three aspects of *context*—the things that happen in addition to what teams do in terms of behavior during actual crises—that sets teams up for success in dealing with crisis situations.

A WORD ABOUT TEAM CRISIS TRAINING

The third issue of context we've mentioned here—team crisis training—plays such a critical double role for teams facing crisis situations, we'll discuss it both here and again in more detail in Chapter 13. Crisis-prepared organizations engage in *anticipatory preparedness* when they go the extra mile and try to anticipate what crises might happen to them by imagining crises that have never happened before. They also engage in anticipatory preparedness when they design and implement crisis management training for the teams that are likely to be integral in responding to such unique, unexpected events. Typically, such training involves designing and implementing realistic, real-time simulated crisis events that may be run for specific teams, for departments or divisions, or for the entire organization within which teams are embedded. And given that many boards of directors are now demanding that management teams institute crisis training and preparation for their organizations (or at the very least for top management teams), there is certainly no shortage of consulting firms ready to help design and run crisis management simulations of every shape and size.

Why would team-level crisis training be so important in distinguishing crisis-prepared from crisis-prone organizations? First, it is one thing to imagine what crisis event might happen; it's another thing entirely to imagine "what would we do" if a never-seen-before crisis event happened. Next, it is practically a quantum leap in preparedness to *practice* the actual behaviors one might need during such a crisis event. Finally, it is *still* a qualitatively different learning experience to practice the actual behaviors *alongside one's own team members* (whether it is in a permanent team of people familiar with one another or in a temporary team of people who have just met) doing the same thing, learning what it would be like to coordinate and communicate with them during that stressful crisis situation.

The team-level "muscle memory" created during such crisis event training is transferable to a real event; additionally, even though, yes, people know that they are participating in a simulated experience, they also experience stress and time pressure during well-designed crisis simulations, and gain valuable feedback about their behaviors afterward. These experiences—just like many military basic training exercises—help desensitize team members and may lessen the perceived threat they experience during real events, allowing them to avoid some of the negative cognitive effects of crisis situations we mentioned earlier.

But there is another, more profound implication of designing and providing meaningful crisis training not only for the teams likely to be on the front lines during critical situations, but for everyone impacted in an organization. Setting aside the time, resources, and management willpower to engage in thoughtful crisis training is the ethical and moral thing to do for the people and teams in the organization, for the community surrounding the organization, and for the stakeholders connected to the organization. Given what we know today about the vortex of uncertainty created by economic, political, environmental, and malicious forces and the likelihood of unpredictable crises to be encountered in the future, it is simply unconscionable that the leaders of an organization would adopt a "sink or swim" policy for its participants, subjecting them to facing the stress of crisis after crisis without providing adequate training. Not only does this sad approach damage individuals and teams, it also damages the families they take their stress home to, as well as the communities they participate in. But we will have much more to say on this topic in Chapter 15.

In the next chapter, we begin our journey into understanding high-performing team behavior during crisis situations. What do these teams do that other teams do not? If you work with or in teams, how can you use this information in your own situation or with those teams and team members you train?

PART I

SETTING THE TONE FOR A CRISIS RESPONSE

Why Are the First Few Minutes Critical for Team Success?

CHAPTER 2

TONE, TIMING, AND PATTERNS

The United States launched Apollo 13, its third lunar mission, in April 1970. En route to its target, one of the spacecraft's oxygen tanks exploded, critically damaging the command module Odyssey. As the popular 1995 feature film Apollo 13 *portrayed, mission control was composed of a team of extremely dedicated specialists who were empowered with the flexibility and authority—even if they were junior team members—to creatively and collaboratively problem solve, especially during crises. As a result, a variety of ideas could be shared and might be scrutinized, but not ignored or undercut in this environment.[1]*

* * *

Apollo 13 Flight Director Gene Kranz, while clearly providing the leadership and structure needed during this crisis, also made sure that *others'* voices and expertise received critical attention in fashioning the best possible team response. If this had been a huge departure from Kranz's normal leadership style, made midstream during a crisis, the likelihood of junior team members speaking up and sharing novel ideas would have been strikingly low, even given the high stakes. However, as will be discussed later, evidence suggests that this was no departure. Kranz had already carefully engaged in *setting the tone* for this team, and by doing so, had facilitated the kind of team interaction that resulted in bringing the Apollo 13 crew safely home.

TONE AND INTERACTION PATTERNS

The concept of "setting the tone" for a team can mean many things to many people. Often, people refer to setting the tone as creating certain emotions in a team—typically, to attempt to create positive feelings or a positive mood in a team as a way to facilitate other things, like collaborative problem-solving. How many times have people brought donuts to a team meeting in the hope of creating a positive tone, or at least a temporarily positive sugar high?

However, in a crisis situation, stress is likely to be very high among team members. Although leaders should probably avoid appearing openly morose or defeatist, there may be limits to their ability to significantly influence the team mood during a crisis. Unlike many of the heartfelt scenarios depicted in the movies, using a "pep talk" in an attempt to change the team's emotions may not always make a significant difference in how well the team actually responds to the impending crisis. Helping a team accurately understand a crisis situation may certainly lessen stress by helping team members gain perspective; sugar-coating the situation or trying to pump up team members' emotions may not help—and could backfire if the team is facing a threatening situation and sees an emotional appeal as out of place.

For example, imagine an emergency department team inundated with critically ill patients during its shift at the beginning of the COVID-19 pandemic. Based on our conversations with members of many such teams, it was clear that they and their organizations were facing an enormous crisis. Although messages of interpersonal support and kindness were welcomed, early attempts from administrators to bolster the emotions of these teams were often seen as inadequate and falling flat; what the teams wanted, we heard, was more opportunity to participate and quickly collaborate in order to revamp processes and procedures suddenly made obsolete by this crisis. Teams wanted more voice in the creation of new interaction and work patterns as this situation unfolded.

Researchers often refer to crises as "strong situations." These situations tend to temporarily override and outweigh other factors, such as personality or even ongoing personal conflicts that might normally contribute to team mood. As with the teams facing the COVID crisis, many interpersonal conflicts fell away as dealing with the crisis took precedence. Given this, and based on our research and observations, we define *setting the tone* here in a very specific and different way, apart from emotion or mood.

Rather than referring to emotion, we refer to setting the tone in terms of influencing the early *patterns of interaction* that emerge among team members during a crisis. Team interaction patterns are defined as regular sets of verbal and nonverbal actions that repeat over time and that are intended for collective action and coordination in a team.[2] These repeated sets of verbalizations or actions usually emerge automatically in teams; occasionally, teams are aware of a pattern, but most of the time, the patterns emerge without the awareness of team members who are concentrated on the immediate tasks at hand. This is particularly true during a crisis situation, when things are changing rapidly and the team members are struggling to respond quickly and accurately. During the fog of a crisis, and particularly early on when things can be very ambiguous, a team may be completely unaware that a particular interaction pattern has emerged.

For example, "talking to the room" is an interaction pattern in which team members shout out newly acquired information to the rest of the team and assume that the person who needs the information will hear it. Members of the U.S. NEADS (Northeast Air Defense Sector) team, charged with monitoring airspace around the northeastern U.S. corridor, engaged in this interaction pattern, among others, on 9/11 in order to quickly share incoming information with team members as the incredibly dynamic, unprecedented events of that day rapidly unfolded.[3] In general, a "talking to the room" interaction pattern might never be explicitly discussed by a team or even noticed; it may simply be a pattern that emerges as the behavior is repeated and adopted into use during a crisis.

These early, emergent patterns are extremely important in teams facing crises. Once they are established, they tend to stick, and they drive team behavior—sometimes for better and other times for worse. Why is it that these interaction patterns emerge in the first place and then persist in teams? Psychological research suggests several reasons. First, we tend to (often unwittingly) import patterns or fragments of patterns we have observed or experienced in previous teams under similar circumstances. Second, we feel more *comfortable* interacting and coordinating with team members when our interactions with them are more predictable; because of this comfort with predictability, we are motivated—again, often unknowingly—to repeat sequences of interactions or actions with each other. Third, we may simply acquiesce to a pattern and thus encourage its repetition; for example, if one team member tends to dominate team briefings or huddles, we may, in a de facto manner, allow the domination pattern to continue after a few failed attempts at changing it.

TIMING MATTERS

In addition to the fact that interaction patterns in teams tend to emerge in an automatic way, research indicates that interaction patterns and action routines emerge extremely *quickly* in teams as soon as they form or begin a new phase of work together. And these patterns and routines tend to be very *persistent* over time, very similar to our own individual habits that resist change. In fact, like those "first impressions" that we form of other people and they form of us upon our first encounters, interaction patterns in teams begin to form *within the first few minutes* of interaction among team members during a crisis.

This might seem fairly intuitive with some thought. Along with all the first impressions that we form of individuals when we meet them, we also fall into patterns of interactions with them very quickly. After just a few minutes of conversation with a new acquaintance, people can report their feelings about that individual regarding liking, trust, attraction, and a host of other factors (think "speed dating" here). These impressions are influenced by perceptions and feelings of *rapport* that result from interpersonal interaction patterns of reciprocity (or turn-taking during conversation), listening, nonverbal behavior such as nodding, eye contact, and many others. Likewise, within the first few minutes of team interaction, an impartial outside observer could quickly identify patterns that emerged in a team facing a crisis—for example, if team members interrupt each other, if female team members tend to be interrupted, if team members pause to make summary statements, if team members ignore or discount information held by only one team member, or if team members react negatively to others' suggestions. These interaction patterns emerge in a milieu that consists of the differences and preferences of the individuals in the team, of how team members influence each other, and of the crisis situation itself.

Recall the fairly benign example of an early-emerging team interaction pattern that we suggested in Chapter One—that is, team members showing up for weekly team meetings and automatically sitting in the same chair at each meeting. If you happen to be late for one of those meetings and find someone in your usual chair, you may feel a twinge of frustration or annoyance at having your comfortable, predictable routine upset. You may even be a little short in your interactions with the teammate who "stole" your seat, but you may not consciously process the reason.

This seating arrangement is a form of interaction pattern that emerged quickly and automatically in the team, and that has consequences for effectiveness and other team outcomes. Seating arrangements in the team may influence power, information sharing, and the emergence of other interaction patterns that, in turn, also influence team effectiveness. In fact, there is some research evidence that the interaction pattern of *sitting* during the briefings rather than standing may negatively influence decision speed and quality.[4] Other research suggests that virtual teams with a pattern of participative team interaction have members who perceive higher levels of information sharing and effectiveness in their teams.[5]

It should become clear at this point that given the complexities of team members and crisis situations, myriad interaction patterns might emerge within the first few minutes of a team's work together. Teams are often unaware of this, instead thinking that everything that occurs in a team during a team's lifespan carries equal weight. This thinking is incorrect, as those interaction patterns emerging within the first few minutes are likely to stick and influence a team's subsequent work together. The good news is that—with this awareness—team leaders and members can help *proactively shape* a team's early interaction patterns and *increase team effectiveness*. Rather than leaving the emergence of early interaction pattern development completely to chance, team members can act to help shape those early interaction patterns into a more precise style during those first few minutes that the team is together.

Together with our research partners, we conducted three studies that help us identify ways to shape early team interaction patterns that result in more effective team outcomes in crisis situations. In Chapter 3, we describe studies of trauma teams and flight crews, and how their interactions during their first few minutes together as a team predict their later behaviors during critical

situations. In Chapter 4, we describe studies of commercial seaport crisis teams
and MBA student teams, and how their earlier patterns of interaction during
task performance influence their subsequent effectiveness handling simulated
crisis events.

THE RESEARCH

The studies described in Chapters 3 and 4 detail empirical research conducted with teams known as "swift-starting action teams." These are multidisciplinary teams of trained team members who come together and coordinate
their efforts during a critical event. The teams are referred to as "swift-starting"
teams because team members may or may not have worked together before the
event; even if they have no experience working together, they are still expected
to quickly form as a team, have the training necessary to know and perform
their roles, and communicate and coordinate effectively to address the situation. These teams do not have time for the old "forming/storming/norming/
performing/adjourning" group development model that appears on the pages
of just about every management textbook in the world; in fact, if their effectiveness depended on taking time to pass through all these phases of group
development, then the well-being of the people and organizations these teams
protect would surely suffer for it.

By collecting and analyzing data from swift-starting teams, we were able to
identify which patterns emerged early in the teams' activity that had positive
effects on later team performance. But does this mean that our research only
pertains to swift-starting teams? What about an ongoing team that has been
working together for a couple of years? There is plenty of research evidence to
suggest that even for ongoing teams, a crisis event provides a dramatic enough
shock to act as a "pause" for many of a team's ongoing interaction patterns.
Researchers have identified similar moments in teams facing unexpected or
stressful situations referred to variously as punctuated equilibria, exogenous
shocks, discontinuous events, or transition phases. While they may not provide exactly the same situation as a new swift-starting team coming together
completely fresh, the shock of a crisis situation still provides the ongoing team
with a solid and natural motivation to disengage from many old interaction
patterns, and new interaction patterns will quickly emerge. For example, after

the Apollo 1 disaster, in which the three astronaut crew members died in a cockpit fire during a practice launch, NASA Flight Director Gene Kranz recalled that he immediately and effectively "reset" his team with a new tone. After the disaster, Kranz told his team that they all—including himself—had avoided responsibility and accountability by not calling off the mission if and when they felt that something was not quite right. In effect, he told them, they had not been tough enough to do everything right. After that point, Kranz told each team member to write "Tough and Competent" on the blackboard of every office in order to set a "framework" for the team until they landed a person on the moon.[6]

Thus, the tone of shared accountability, along with the ability and expectation to speak up, and the goals of "tough and competent" were set (or reset) in the Apollo team. By so clearly setting the tone after this exogenous shock, Kranz molded the team's subsequent interaction patterns that allowed it to innovate and quickly create novel solutions during the later Apollo 13 crisis. Just like "shocks" and "crises" in our personal lives lead us to reflect and provide us the opportunity to "reset" priorities and behaviors, they can function similarly for teams.

In the next chapter, we turn to the first two of four published research studies that illustrate critical aspects of setting the tone. The first study details how differences in setting the tone were connected to performance outcomes in hospital trauma teams. This research explores the idea of "communication balance" as a way for team members and leaders to set the tone in a team before potential critical situations arise. The second study examines behaviors used in flight crews to set the tone before flying a simulated leg of flight, and how those tone-setting behaviors corresponded with crew performance later during unexpected critical events. Taken together, these studies give us a good look at the power of early tone-setting in teams and how these efforts may correspond with better outcomes when critical situations arise.

CHAPTER 3

HOW TRAUMA TEAMS
AND FLIGHT CREWS
SET THE TONE

T HE PREVIOUS CHAPTER DETAILS THE NOTION of "setting the tone" and why it is so critical for teams facing crisis situations. In order to better understand the differences in setting the tone between lower- and higher-performing teams during stressful, uncertain tasks, we examined these behaviors in emergency medicine trauma teams and in aviation flight crews. Would trauma teams and flight crews that excelled in setting the tone during their first few minutes together actually perform better when later faced with unexpected, critical situations? While we only studied two types of teams here, it is fairly straightforward to imagine our results mapping onto similar types of teams, such as firefighters, SWAT teams, military teams, and other teams in organizations, such as project teams or top management teams—in general, any type of team that has well-trained members performing specific roles, and that may face unexpected, critical events.

One thing that sets these two studies apart from the other "setting the tone" studies we will discuss next in Chapter 4 is the timing of the behaviors we studied. Due to the complexity of their work as well as the fact that team members often do not know each other, members of both trauma teams and flight crews come together for quick briefings—for some teams only a few minutes in duration—before jumping into their complex team taskwork together. Given this, we focused on how the teams set the tone specifically during these briefing periods when the teams were first coming together. Doing so gives us a special view into the power and influence of setting the tone while a team is forming and before it engages in its taskwork.

STUDY 1: TRAUMA TEAMS[1]

The Setting. This study was led by Dr. Lillian Su, MD, and involved her colleagues at a large U.S. pediatric hospital. These clinicians and medical researchers video-recorded real trauma teams as they worked together during simulated trauma situations. In our study, the twelve separate nine-member trauma teams each worked through four simulated trauma situations, creating a total of forty-seven simulation videos (one video of the original forty-eight was damaged and not used in the study).

Trauma teams are swift-starting, multidisciplinary teams of healthcare workers who coordinate their efforts to treat a severely injured patient. Typical trauma team composition includes a lead physician, a surgical resident, an anesthesiologist, a critical care or emergency room physician, a bedside nurse, a recording nurse, a medication nurse, and a respiratory therapist. The team members first assemble while the patient is in transit in the ambulance or helicopter. Usually, the trauma team receives important information about the patient from the emergency medical technicians (EMTs) during these few minutes before the patient's arrival at the hospital. This information allows them to prepare both themselves and the trauma room.

When we describe the trauma teams as responding to "simulated" traumas, we mean something very different from the type of computer-based or virtual reality headset game-type simulation one might see these days. Although the teams knew they were participating in a research study, the physicians, nurses, and therapists in the teams took the simulations and their performance in them *very* seriously; after all, well-designed, high-fidelity simulations are expensive to design, equip, and run, *and* the participants were performing in front of their peers and colleagues. The simulations were held in an actual trauma room (or "bay") in the hospital, furnished with the equipment, monitors, lighting, and medicines normally found there. The "patients" were high-fidelity computerized manikins that breathed, blinked, and indicated vital signs and symptoms as if they were real patients; additionally, the manikins exhibited programmed symptoms that correlated with the scenario scripts, and they responded to the teams' treatments and decisions as one would expect real patients would.

We focused our research on how the interaction tone was set in trauma teams during these first few minutes as the team assembled and awaited their "patient," who was en route to the hospital. As we will describe, the trauma teams in our study that achieved the best outcomes were the ones that set the tone during the short initial waiting period in very different ways as compared to the other teams.

Study Design. In each simulation, the trauma team worked together to identify and treat two potentially life-threatening situations, such as hypotension, pneumothorax, seizure, and profound hypothermia. We analyzed the video recordings of the teams working through these simulations and noted each time team members engaged in certain key interactions such as: requesting information, providing information as requested, giving an opinion or advice, asking for permission, providing unsolicited information, giving a direct command, and giving an indirect command. Then we calculated two important indicators of team health: *communication balance* and *implicit co-ordination*. We used communication balance to characterize the initial interaction patterns so crucial in setting the tone during that initial period before patient arrival, and anticipation ratio to characterize the effectiveness of the team process that occurred after the patient arrival, when the team worked to treat the patient's injuries. Table 4 lists a sample of the behaviors we coded from the video recordings.

Concerning communication balance, just as healthy interpersonal relationships are characterized by reciprocal interactions and a high amount of back-and-forth exchange in conversation, with both individuals participating fairly equally, research indicates that back-and-forth reciprocity in team interaction is also related to team effectiveness. Have you ever met someone for the first time, and that person started dominating the conversation right away? You could not get a word in edgewise. It certainly set the tone and interaction pattern for the remainder of the conversation, and quite possibly the remainder of all your interactions with that particular individual, and not in a good way. Communication balance is a measure of that type of reciprocity in teams; if one

TABLE 4.   List of Sample Coded Behaviors

Behavior	Definition	Example
Information request	A request for information or verification	Do you hear any breath sounds?
Information request response	A response to a request for information	No, no breath sounds.
Permission request	A request for permission to complete an action	Can I start the secondary survey now?
Provide action/ patient information	A provision of unsolicited information	Blood pressure is 60 over 36.
Direct command	A command given; the actor clearly conveys what needs to be done and by whom	Reassess breath sounds for us, [name of team member].
Indirect command	A command given; the actor is not clear in either what needs to be done or by whom	He needs another 800 cc bolus.

person dominates the interactions in the team by hijacking the early conversation with monologues, the communication balance (and variance of speaking across team members) is high, and is likely to stay high. In this case, high is bad because it means that one or two people are quite different from the rest of the team and are taking up more airtime. On the other hand, if everyone is encouraged to speak and feels free to do so, the communication balance (and variance of speaking across team members) is low, and is likely to stay low.

In our study, we measured communication balance in the teams during that brief initial period as teams prepared for the arrival of their patient. In some teams, the lead physician brought team members together during those short few minutes before patient arrival and encouraged all team members to share ideas about how best to prepare for the situation, resulting in balanced communication (low variance). In other teams, the lead physician brought team members together and launched into a monologue expressing what they saw as the main goals of the team, likely problems they would face with the patient, and what each member should prepare for in the next few minutes (high variance). Or, sometimes, another team member or a pair of team members seemed to dominate this vital initial conversation. These differences may have occurred due to differences in training, personality, and the mix of people on the team, or were likely due to a combination of factors; however, the aim of our study was not to understand *why* these differences occurred, but instead to find out if they led to important downstream effects in team behavior and effectiveness later as the team's tasks became more complex.

One such downstream behavior is *implicit coordination*, which we measured beginning after the patient arrived. Implicit coordination—an important characteristic of an effective swift-starting team—is the ability of members to anticipate each other's needs. It is, in fact, the very essence of a team acting as the proverbial "well-oiled machine." Just imagine how unwieldy a team would be if every time a team member needed a piece of information or part of a task from a colleague, they had to explicitly ask for it. Instead, most swift-starting teams are populated with professional, expert team members who not only do their own jobs but also have a sense for when a colleague might need some information or a tool, and provide them without being asked. When this "sensing" is done again and again by multiple team members, it constitutes implicit coordination and helps make the team more smooth and efficient in its overall efforts.

Results. Our analysis revealed that the teams with more balanced communication during the initial period before the patient arrived engaged in higher levels of implicit coordination after the patient arrived and they treated the patient's injuries. What did this look like? Some teams had lead physicians who set the tone during the pre-arrival period by asking questions, inviting comments, listening well—in general, by giving everyone else on the team the opportunity to engage in those back-and-forth, reciprocal interactions. Such interactions quickly solidified into trust-based interaction patterns that the teams carried with them as they moved into the more stressful phase of treating a patient with critical injuries. And these patterns facilitated the implicit coordination that we measured.

Did these teams with leaders who set the tone with more balanced communication outperform other teams? Our analysis revealed that the more a team member (likely the lead physician) spoke during the pre-arrival period (that is, the *less balanced* the team communication), the *lower* the implicit coordination was in the team after the pre-arrival period and the *longer* the team took to perform a critical medical intervention—such as administering a life-saving medication—for the patient. Presumably, teams in which members shared ideas and expressed opinions before the patient arrived addressed the plans and contingencies that would be relevant during treatment—thus allowing for faster interventions. In contrast, teams where one or two members dominated the pre-arrival briefing did not benefit from those reciprocal interaction patterns and implicit coordination when problems arose, and this likely resulted in their slower interventions. So the next time you or a loved one faces a medical procedure from a team, make sure the team comes together and *sets the tone* with *balanced communication.*

With these considerations in mind, at the end of the chapter we present strategies for establishing balanced communication during initial interactions. These are practices derived from the scholarly literature and from our own observations of many teams. One may implement them in initial one-on-one interactions and during early team briefings. Obviously, not every practice is necessary—or even appropriate—in every circumstance. The particulars of the crisis context matter. Still, we hope team members and leaders find some useful strategies to leverage when a crisis occurs—and, as discussed in Chapter 13, in training for crises.

STUDY 2: FLIGHT CREWS[2]

The Setting. For this study, we worked with our colleagues Dr. Fred Zijlstra and Sybil Phillips to collect and examine data from eighteen newly formed two-person flight crews as they came together to prepare for their upcoming training flight. As with the trauma teams, these team conversations were the first moments of the teams' work together but didn't involve actually doing their assigned task—that is, cooperatively flying the aircraft; instead, these pre-task periods, also known as the flight preparation phase or preflight briefing, were part of the crews' flight simulator training session conducted as part of a semester-long aviation course at a large U.S. university. The simulator was a computer-controlled, stationary flight simulator that mimicked the reactions of the actual aircraft the pilots would later fly together. The "pilot flying" (often referred to as the Captain) sat at the left-hand controls, and the "pilot not flying" (often referred to as the First Officer) sat at the right-hand controls; both pilots shared and traded flight tasks as necessary during this high-taskload training exercise. The pilots all held their private pilot licenses and were enrolled in a Crew Resource Management course that focused on training them how to fly larger twin-engine aircraft cooperatively as a crew. The pilots' interactions during the flight preparation phase would set the tone for their ensuing flight together.

Study Design. The crews' flight preparation conversations as well as their subsequent task performance in their simulated flight were video-recorded, similar to the trauma team study. Using the videos, we coded the incidence of key crew behaviors (very similar to the behaviors coded for the trauma teams) during their flight preparation phase—that is, from the time the pilots arrived at the simulator until they received clearance for takeoff—and examined this early portion of their pre-task communication for "setting the tone" evidence and interaction patterns. The average duration for the preflight phase was seventeen minutes. In our analyses, we looked for evidence that crews' early flight preparation communication patterns predicted their later task performance during their simulated flight. That flight performance was rated by aviation experts using an industry-standard checklist.

Results. For our analyses, we used the pattern recognition algorithm Theme (www.patternvision.com) to help characterize the interaction patterns of the crews during their flight preparation phase. We looked for significant differences in flight preparation interaction patterns between the lower- and higher-performing flight crews. What we found was remarkably similar to our trauma team results.

We found that those teams with flight preparation conversation patterns characterized with high levels of reciprocity and stability (both in terms of duration and complexity) were more likely to be higher-performing crews. Why might this be true? First, high levels of reciprocity likely created the same higher levels of psychological safety and fair balance in communication that we discussed regarding the trauma teams and communication balance. One pilot was not dominating the conversation; instead, there was a healthy back-and-forth during the flight preparation conversation, likely with higher levels of pertinent information and ideas exchanged. Second, higher performing crews had flight preparation interaction patterns that quickly settled into predictable, stable levels of duration and complexity. Have you ever had a conversation with someone that feels off-balance and stilted? In these types of conversations, it seems as if you are unable to anticipate when the other person is going to speak, or for how long. More comfortable exchanges fall into predictable rhythms, allowing parties to concentrate more on the information and less on trying to slow down or keep up with the other person.

These two factors—reciprocity and predictability—emerged quickly as the higher performing crews set the tone during their flight preparation conversations. Our practical takeaways based on these results as well as the results from the trauma team study appear in the table at the end of this chapter.

Given the consequences of initial team interactions for later team functioning, understanding how to convert this knowledge into practice when crises occur is important for team leaders. As we have emphasized, the first interactions typically create the norms for later ones. This is because once they are set, early interaction patterns are difficult to change. An analogy we have found useful here is that of laying quick-set concrete. Once set, the concrete is stable; most change—in the form of wear and tear—takes place gradually over a very long stretch of time. So it is with team interaction; once those initial norms of interacting are set, they tend to endure. When sudden and dramatic change does occur—both to the concrete and in how the team interacts—it is usually the result of something going wrong (e.g., a heavy load dropped and significantly altering the concrete, or dramatic team conflict over team functioning). In either case, it is generally to be avoided.

If creating the right norms initially is so important, how does one actually do it? We do not pretend this is easy. When a crisis strikes, the priority is addressing it immediately. We understand that team interaction patterns are likely not a top priority. Also complicating matters is whatever history—or lack of history—that accompanies the team to these early interactions. In some cases, team members collaborate regularly, perhaps even as part of a standing crisis team. Here, norms already exist. Sometimes these norms are desirable, and only need reinforcing during an initial briefing. At other times, the team already follows harmful norms and allows one person to dominate the conversation, while others are hesitant to speak. History works against the team; establishing different norms will be more challenging but is also more important. In still other cases—as is often the case in trauma team settings—team members may have a combination of limited or no history of working with each other. This can be favorable, but it also presents challenges; the team may simply default to the most extroverted, opinionated, or senior person present, and the opportunity to set the tone with balanced communication may be lost.

Taking these two studies together—trauma teams and flight crews—we can offer some practical strategies regarding setting the tone. First, given the consequences of initial team interactions for later team functioning, understanding how to convert this knowledge into practice when crises occur is important, particularly for team leaders. As we have emphasized, the first interactions typically create the norms for later ones. This is because once they are set, patterns are difficult to change. Like the trauma team study, the flight crew study showed that balanced (i.e., reciprocal) communication during the initial briefing was associated with better team functioning. But beyond this, results also showed that having predictable interactions during the preflight briefing was important. Team members benefited from knowing how the interaction would flow—who would be talking when and for how long, at what points they themselves would speak, and so forth. Part of the reason this predictability helps in these early interactions is because members do not need to worry about whether or when they will have the opportunity to speak. It is no longer a competition. Members are already cognitively taxed, and perhaps stressed, while thinking about the upcoming event. By minimizing competition for floor time and anxiety about trying to voice their opinions and information, such predictability allows team members to better focus on their own and others' thoughts about the crisis itself—as they should. We will have more to say about the harmful dynamics of such competitions in a later chapter.

In offering these recommendations, we also need to emphasize two additional points. First, how a team leader or member prepares for and enacts these recommendations may depend on whether this is an unplanned or planned briefing. For many crises, briefings are unplanned; they are ad hoc and occur on the spot; in trauma settings, they generally occur immediately before the patient arrives—or sometimes as the team begins treating the patient. The particulars of the situation (including the composition of the team) are not known in advance, and the time until the team begins addressing the crisis directly (i.e., the patient arrives) is very limited. In other cases—like the flight crews—the briefing is more structured, with checklists to follow. Briefings occur before commercial aviation flights, during which pilots discuss any foreseeable problems for the upcoming flight. There often is ample time before and during the briefing to enact structured interactions, such as those suggested by Crew Resource Management principles.

A second point that we will elaborate on in the following chapters is that the patterned and predictable interaction that benefits teams during initial briefings generally is *not* the type of interaction that will help the team when they are in the throes of the crisis (e.g., when the patient goes into shock, or the aircraft experiences a sudden mechanical failure). As we will discuss, very different interaction types are helpful when a team is directly combating the crisis. It is important teams recognize—and communicate—that different communication norms are helpful during different phases of the crisis. We have much more to say about this in the following chapters.

Practical Takeaways for Chapter 3

- Remember that early interactions happen fast and set the stage for subsequent team functioning.
- Be deliberate in creating and structuring early interactions accordingly.
- Ensure balanced communication during the earliest interactions.
- Make it known that everyone's perspective is important and will be heard.
- During a planned, pre-crisis briefing, establish consistency and predictability in interactions.
- Develop and implement ground rules for the briefing to establish such consistency.
- Communicate that interaction norms during briefings can (and likely should) differ from those that occur when the team is engaged in the crisis.

CHAPTER 4

HOW SEAPORT AND MBA CRISIS TEAMS SHARE INFORMATION AND AVOID SOLUTION FIXATION

A S WE DESCRIBED IN CHAPTER 3, THE TRAUMA teams we studied that achieved more communication balance in their first few minutes together before their patient arrived were able to use more implicit coordination and perform better later on when things became critical. Similarly, the flight crews that made their flight preparation conversations more reciprocal and stable ended up outperforming other crews on their subsequent flying tasks. Taken together, and with time-pressured teams performing complex tasks in critical situations, these two studies show us how very important setting the tone can be.

In this final chapter in our Setting the Tone section, we will share evidence from two additional research studies. Both of these studies show how the early interactions of teams influences their later ability to handle critical situations; however, the teams we describe here differ from the Chapter 3 trauma teams and flight crews in two important ways. First, rather than focusing on teams as they come together for the first time to work on a task together, the teams we describe here are composed of members who know each other and who have very likely worked with each other on similar tasks in the past. Second, rather than focus chiefly on the teams' interactions before they begin working on their tasks, we focus here on a longer duration of teams' interactions that continue on after they have begun their work together, expanding our view past an initial briefing period.

At the end of this chapter, we summarize our research evidence for setting the tone and offer more practical advice on how to use what we've learned through this research.

EXAMPLE 1: SEAPORT CRISIS TEAMS[1]

Our third example of setting the tone involves a study of crisis management teams that was led by Dr. Sjir Uitdewilligen of Maastricht University in the Netherlands. These crisis management teams were made up of professionals assembled specifically to handle crisis events. The twelve teams in the study were multidisciplinary crisis management teams at the Port of Rotterdam— one of the busiest commercial ports in the world.

The Setting. At the time of the study, the Port of Rotterdam and its adjacent industrial area stretched over 25 miles and covered 26,000 acres. It encompassed multiple oil refineries, chemical facilities, and terminals for gas, oil, chemical, and edible oil and fat producers. Considering the enormous volume of activity handled by the port and its close proximity to a densely populated urban area, the situation at the port was perpetually vulnerable to a wide variety of unpredictable crisis events.

All members of the teams in the study were active employees of the port or of stakeholder emergency services and were individuals who might be called upon in reality to serve on a crisis management team during an actual crisis at the port. Each nine-member multidisciplinary team was led by an officer of the fire brigade and was comprised of an additional officer of the fire brigade, an officer of the police force, an officer of the port authority, a chemical specialist from the environmental protection service, a representative of the medical emergency service, a representative of the municipality, an information manager, and a public relations official of the police department. The study crisis team members were assigned to these ad hoc teams based on their work schedules and availability, as they would be for real crisis management teams.

Study Design. The crisis management teams were observed and video-recorded as they performed a regularly scheduled training exercise. This consisted of a simulated scenario of an incident comparable in severity and complexity to the type of incidents they would encounter in their roles as team members during crisis management operations in the port. Examples of possible crises at the port include chemical leakages on a cargo ship, a fire at a chemical plant, and large-scale accidents involving chemicals. The scenario used for the study was developed by industry experts working with representatives from the various emergency services. Team members sat together in a room resembling a control room they would use during an actual crisis. Each team member sat at an individual workstation that provided access to information from colleagues in the field near the crisis site, databases, and the Internet, and that also provided communication with other team members and simulation trainers. At regular intervals, team members came together in the corner of the room at a rectangular table to share information, construct a shared understanding of the situation, and collectively make decisions. The training exercise was developed to reflect the actual task situation the teams could face in the field as closely as possible. Overall, the setting and the messaging and communication system were similar to what teams would experience during real crises at the port.

Researchers collected data from video recordings of the teams. Periodically, as team members met in the corner of the control room, they shared information, planned, and made decisions about how to move forward in handling the crisis, which for this scenario involved a serious traffic accident resulting in multiple casualties and a chemical spill. Multiple simulation instructors rated the performance of each team on a variety of dimensions after the simulation ended.

Results. For this study, we used a wider temporal lens to examine setting the tone; rather than focus exclusively on *initial* interaction patterns, analyses here focused on sequential phases of behavior unfolding over a longer period of time in these teams. Based on the analyses of the video recordings of twelve crisis management teams as they worked through the complex crisis simulation (with an average duration of three hours), three separate phases of activity emerged. These phases were identified using a painstakingly precise method of behavioral coding developed by Dr. Uitdewilligen.

The first phase, *structuring*, involved the team clarifying team members' roles and creating ground rules about communication and meetings. The second phase, *information sharing*, involved team members sharing and pooling relevant pieces of information with each other and augmenting information with added details and insights. The final phase, *decision making*, involved team members making functional decisions vital for the team's coordination and operations.

After all the behavioral coding and statistical analyses were finished, and team performance was measured by industry experts, the data showed two striking differences between low- and high-performing teams concerning their early interaction patterns. First, compared to other teams, higher-performing teams spent significantly *longer* time in the *early structuring phase*. While other teams seemed to jump into the problem feetfirst with very little effort given to structuring activities, high-performing teams seemed to approach the crisis situation knowing that if all team members weren't on the "same page" from the beginning, coordination would become problematic as things became more complex. These teams chose early on to invest the necessary time in making sure that all team members understood the basic frameworks and assumptions necessary in the coordination of tasks and communication *before* diving into the issues. You might think of this as setting the tone, but in a more prospective way. In essence, these teams were building team mental models[2]—shared cognitive representations of the team's work environment and how the team would work together. This finding is very consistent with the trauma study and the flight crew study in that this early structuring very much helped set the tone right away and facilitated better collaborative decision making later on when things became more complex.

Second, higher-performing crisis teams spent more time than other teams in the *information sharing phase*—starting early, after structuring—digging into information, sharing it across team members, and discussing it deeply. This is quite similar to what Carsten De Dreu has described as "motivated information processing," meaning the motivation that team members have to share information increases as their perception increases that the team outcome depends on their cooperative interdependence.[3] This deeper information processing was very likely a by-product of teams' earlier prospective tone-setting; because these team members understood how their roles fit together, what information each person would likely have and need, and how truly interdependent they were, they were more motivated to notice, gather, share, ask for, and discuss information.

So higher-performing crisis teams took the time early on to structure the situation and to really dig into the information at hand. This in-task (as opposed to pre-task) effort to set the tone in their teams resulted in decision making with more reciprocal sensemaking, where team members collaboratively build on one another's ideas. Ultimately, the ideas and decisions of these teams benefited greatly from how the team's work began early on—that is, by setting the tone.

EXAMPLE 2: MBA CRISIS TEAMS[4]

The final example of setting the tone involves one of the few studies we will describe that does not involve team members in performing tasks that they might perform on their real jobs. This study, led by Dr. Serena Sohrab, focused on teams composed of MBA students as they worked during a crisis decision-making simulation. Does the fact that these are student teams make the knowledge gained less valuable? We do not believe so; in fact, because many factors could be controlled in this simulation and because the sample of teams—twenty-eight of them—was larger than some of the other studies, there could have been less "noise" and possibility of intervening events that could have affected the results.

The Setting. The crisis task faced by the MBA teams in this study was part of a longer simulation developed by Dr. Amy Edmondson at Harvard University: the Everest Simulation. In this simulation, teams composed of five to seven members each assume the roles of a climbing team on a mission to ascend Mount Everest. The members are given certain unique information, skills, and abilities—for example, one member is a photographer, while another is a long-distance runner. As you can imagine, members must excel in their collaborative and communicative skills in order to achieve this goal as a team, and the simulation makes sure that they face unexpected crisis situations along the way.

Study Design. The teams had already shared information and made decisions in the simulation by the time they encountered the crisis situation that was the focus of this study. We are unsure how the teams set the tone in their first few minutes of time together; however, we can certainly see how the teams handled things differently once the crisis hit. The crisis began when the team learned that one team member had become critically ill, and the members needed to decide as a team what to do. Numerous options were available to each team, and all held different consequences. The asymmetrically distributed information held by team members needed to be thoroughly shared, explored, and discussed by a team in order to arrive at the best solution.

Results. After coding and analyzing the behaviors of the teams from their videos, it quickly became clear that the early actions of higher-performing teams after the crisis began differed significantly from other teams. The difference can be seen in the graphs of the team behaviors for high-, average-, and low-performing teams over the duration of the crisis; the "information phase" in particular pertains to sharing and discussing the available information. Similar to the port crisis teams, higher performers here spent much more time sharing and discussing information first, before offering and weighing potential solutions. Even if someone on the team proposed a potential solution, these

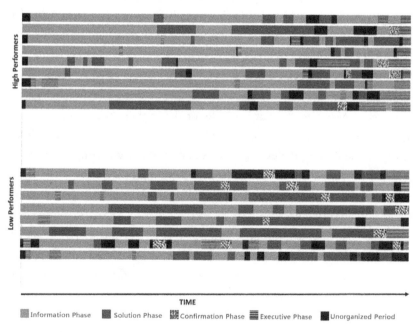

FIGURE I.   High and Low Performers. Permission courtesy of the *Journal of Organizational Behavior.*

teams seemed to sense that it was too early to disengage from understanding the information available—in other words, they set an in-task tone focused on reciprocal, balanced information sharing and discussion. Lower-performing teams, on the other hand, seemed unable to resist talking about potential solutions; the time they devoted to understanding the available information (and thus the crisis) paled in comparison to higher performers. This "solution fixation trap" seemed to draw in the lower performers; once they started talking about possible solutions, they rarely returned to an exploration of the information, and as a result, they based decisions on faulty assumptions or understandings with gaps in coverage.

These takeaways build on the practical recommendations from Chapter 3. Whether in the briefing—before a team begins taking corrective actions—or as a team begins implementing those actions, a team will need to establish a shared mental model. Actually, one might think of a team needing multiple shared mental models. One shared mental model concerns how the team *interacts* during the crisis. As we see in this study and in those from Chapter 3, a team can shape this team process mental model during the earliest team interactions. In the student teams described in this chapter, successful teams very likely spent considerable time ensuring that all members understood the nature of the scenario and how they were to collaborate when interacting during their respective tasks. The establishment of this early mental model likely facilitated a second one, when the team engaged in deep collective information processing. Members did not compete for the "right answer" or take action unilaterally in hopes of becoming the hero. All members knew that their job involved monitoring the evolving crisis and then freely sharing information about the situation without fear of reprise. The mindset of the successful teams reflects that the members are working to diagnose and solve this problem as a collective. Speaking up is not just accepted; it is encouraged. This mindset is important because, despite the team's best first efforts to consider the nature of the crisis and how to handle it, new information will emerge and the crisis will change over time. Thus, again, the initial team interactions pave the way for the latter effective ones. At the end of this section, we provide practical recommendations gleaned from these studies for your teams.

In offering these practical recommendations to avoid rushing to solutions, we want to emphasize that our message is not to pause and deliberate before "stopping the bleeding" as quickly as possible. Quite the contrary. In reality, many crises require two or more sets of phases—and corresponding sets of responses—over time. The first phase (and response) is often an immediate one. Here, implementing certain restorative actions instantly is automatic, and indeed should be. In nuclear power plants, a (potential) meltdown triggers operators to immediately insert the rods that will cease the nuclear reactions. In trauma settings, the team's first priority is to stabilize the patient (e.g., by restoring breathing and heart function) as promptly as possible. We are not suggesting teams deliberate at length about these types of actions.

- Have each team member regularly share their perspectives and their perceived roles:
  - *You can do this during briefings and when there are lulls in the crisis. Regularly ask members what their understanding of the situation is.*
  - *You can train for this during simulations by having each member note their current assessment of the situation. Then have members share these—to assess team convergence and identify holes.*
- Announce a "no criticism" rule for sharing observations and suggestions: Emphasize that the team's goal is to understand and address the scenario.
- Reward members who share observations and information.
- Announce a norm that all comments must be task-related: When disagreements about tasks become (or are perceived as) personal slights, team conflict ensues.
- Have the team generate a list of potential scenarios that are occurring (and potential solutions):
  - *Ideally, each member generates their own list individually to increase the number of possibilities.*
- Acknowledge your own uncertainty about what is happening and what may happen next: This will make others more willing to speak up.
- Prohibit team members from offering solutions when probing about the nature of the scenario: This is a straightforward solution, but in our experience it is also surprisingly challenging for teams to execute.
- Reward generating interpretations about the situation—not just solutions to deal with it: Team members often want to please and impress team leaders. Leverage this by praising members for making observations and offering ideas about what is going on, not only for suggesting corrective actions.
- Model inquisitive behavior: "Think aloud" to model the type of behavior and interaction you wish to elicit. For example, you could state something like, "Well, it seems like X is happening . . . but if that were the case, we would not be seeing Z happen."
- Do not expect to fully identify the causes or nature of the crisis initially: Often, your team will not fully understand the crisis—or corrective actions—after the initial briefing. Crises are complex and change over time. Do not strive for certainty, but rather encourage the team to continue considering and discussing hypotheses about what may be happening.

FIGURE 2.   Strategies for Establishing Predictable Communication Patterns.

It is after initiating these stabilizing actions that many teams fail to then share and consider the information available; instead, they often rush to further solutions when they should more thoroughly consider the underlying nature and causes of the situation they are addressing. In reality, most crises are caused by multiple factors interacting in various ways. Causes often are not manifest but rather are buried deep in complex and intertwined systems (e.g., bodily systems in patients, various units within organizations and their external environments). This "tight-coupling" of complex systems often means that the presenting problem is not the real, underlying problem. It also means that intervening in one system—or in one way—can upset other closely linked aspects of systems. For all these reasons, jumping to implement solutions without carefully sharing and exploring all the information can be ineffectual at a minimum or even disastrous in some cases. As such, we offer practical suggestions for helping your team deliberate sufficiently about the crisis before beginning to implement solutions, especially these latter-stage ones (see Figure 2).

SETTING THE TONE SUMMARY

When we consider all four of these studies—the trauma teams, the flight crews, the port crisis teams, and the MBA crisis teams—what is the overall picture that comes into view of setting the tone? The following table provides an overview of what high-performing teams did early on to succeed in very different crisis contexts.

After watching these teams and countless others similar to them for hundreds of hours, it is clear to us that setting the tone with high levels of participation across team members sets in motion two critical forces in teams that, later on—when things become dynamic, complex, and unpredictable—help explain the performance bifurcation we see in teams dealing with crisis situations. First, early high participation, if reciprocal and balanced, can lead to the sense of belonging, psychological safety, and interpersonal connectedness that promote implicit coordination and helping behavior. Second, early high participation can help create the team mental models—the "same page" shared understanding of how the team works and shared assumptions about the tasks and work situation—that greatly facilitate later coordination efforts as the crisis unfolds.

In order to help teams and team leaders manage the process of setting the tone during that critical initial period, we've created the Setting the Tone

TABLE 5. Setting the Tone Summary

	Early "Setting the Tone" Behaviors	Later Coordination Behaviors	Final Team Outcome
Trauma Teams	Early balanced, reciprocal interaction across team members	Implicit coordination	Significantly faster than other teams to administer critical interventions for patients in simulation
Flight Crews	Early reciprocal interaction patterns consistent in duration and complexity	Implicit coordination, helping behavior	Expert-rated by instructors as effective (standard to outstanding) in preflight, takeoff, cruise, approach, and landing phases of flight
Port Crisis Teams	Early collaborative discussion of members' roles, team communication rules, and assumptions	Collective sensemaking, rapid decision making, using decision visualization	Expert-rated by instructors as exemplary for crisis management in this context
MBA Crisis Teams	Early focus on information sharing and exploration	Putting off premature solution attempts	High-quality decisions grounded in solid understanding of available information

Checklist included here. The checklist covers the material from Chapters 2 through 4. It can be used during the initial period of the crisis as a reminder of the behaviors that set the team up for later success, or as a tool for team reflection after a crisis or training exercise. It also can be used when a team initially forms. We would suggest that spending time on a tool like this will be at least as helpful as a more social/recreational team-building exercise that—while enjoyable—may have little to do with the team's actual tasks. While setting the tone with the behaviors described here is no guarantee of success during an unpredictable, complex event, it typically can't hurt to have everyone rowing, and rowing in the same direction.

In the next section, we focus more intently on what high-performing teams do differently from other teams right in the thick of a crisis event. Again, we draw not from stories or opinions, but from empirical research evidence to share some nonobvious, surprising results.

TABLE 6.   Setting the Tone Checklist

Y or N	Behavioral Marker	Interpretation
	High proportion of team members speak or contribute.	**Y** = More balanced communication and higher likelihood of implicit coordination later *If N . . .* • *Consider asking quieter team members directly for their opinions/insights.* • *If feasible, use an electronic message board (e.g., a Google Doc) in addition to verbal communication. People may feel more comfortable sharing ideas virtually.* • *If a given team member is dominating the communication, ask them what they would like to know from other team members. This can help shift their focus to being more receptive and learning-oriented.* • *Recognize the positive contributions of members. Ensure that the team realizes that the person who speaks the most—or speaks with the most authority—is not always the person who knows the most.*
	Team members do not interrupt each other.	**Y** = More balanced communication; likely more respect felt among team members *If N . . .* • *Set a "no interruptions" norm. Consider setting a team penalty (even a humorous one) or a charitable one (such as donating a dollar to a charity of the group's choice) for each time a member interrupts. This will facilitate team members to "call out" one another without reproach.*
	Team members respond directly to each other's comments.	**Y** = More reciprocity in communication, more efficient coordination later *If N . . .* • *Set a "direct conversation" norm, rather than speaking only to the team leader.* • *Conduct practice exercises where members need to think about who most needs the information they have to impart (before speaking). Within this exercise, also consider setting goals (and/or limits) for how often members speak with one another.*
	Team members feel comfortable sharing ideas and information.	**Y** = Felt psychological safety *If N . . .* • *Set a "no blame" norm for sharing ideas.* • *Frame the crisis as a chance for the team to learn.* • *Acknowledge members who make mistakes while trying to learn.* • *Convey (and enforce) the message that trying to impress you (the leader) runs counter to how you view effective teamwork.*
	The team clarifies who does what.	**Y** = Adequate time in structuring phase, and likely more efficient coordination later. *If N . . .* • *Ensure each person understands their actions during each phase of the ensuing crisis. Have each member describe (or act out) their role. Tabletop and simulation exercises are effective training tools for this.* • *Encourage members to think about their own and others' roles during the crisis. Have them ask, "Is what I'm doing part of my role? What other parts of my role am I not doing? Do I know what my role currently is? If not, how can I seek clarification?"*

Y or N	Behavioral Marker	Interpretation
	The team clarifies ground rules about communication and coordination going forward.	**Y** = Adequate time in structuring phase, and likely more efficient coordination later *If N . . .* • *Create a team contract, adhere to it, and update it when needed.* • *Ensure that the team integrates discussion of communication and coordination into team meetings and briefings. Focus should not just be on the crisis but also (when time permits) on how the team is (and should be) operating. Team debriefings and after-action reviews are beneficial for this.*
	Team members build on each other's ideas.	**Y** = Collaborative sensemaking and likely higher-quality decisions *If N . . .* • *Consider using a shared digital document in addition to verbal communication for exchange of ideas. This can reduce "groupthink" and people interrupting each other when generating ideas.* • *Do not only reward idea generation on the team. Recognize and reward idea implementation (e.g., working out the "small details," addressing barriers when implementing the idea) as well.*

Practical Takeaways for Chapter 4

- Ensure that the <u>team maintains a shared mental model</u>; use briefings for this purpose.

- To the extent possible, encourage thorough team discussion about the crisis (e.g., "What is the nature of it?," "How will we address it?") before the team decides on a single solution and "jumps into action."

- Encourage members to <u>regularly share information and ask questions</u> of each other as they engage with the crisis. Such will increase other members' situational awareness of the evolving crisis.

- Ensure that the team thoroughly <u>discusses the nature of the crisis and potential contingencies before discussing potential solutions</u>.

- Once solutions are discussed (and implemented), <u>continue to assess whether they are the correct ones for the crisis or if you misdiagnosed the scenario</u>.

PART II

ADAPTING ON THE FLY

*What Are the Specific Behaviors Successful
Teams Use to Adapt to Unexpected Crises?*

CHAPTER 5

TO ADAPT . . . WITH ROUTINES OR WITHOUT THEM?

Faced with a much larger and more well-equipped Russian adversary, teams spread throughout the Ukrainian army have shown remarkable adaptivity and innovativeness during the invasion that began in 2022—so much so that they have been referred to as a "MacGyver Army" by the American Legion and others.[1]

Examples of teams able to abandon standard procedures and routines in order to pivot to new methods abound. Teams have both developed and adopted a smartphone app that allows troops in the field to order up artillery strikes with the ease of ordering an Uber. Other teams using 3D printers have turned cheap toy drones into lethal weapons. Still other teams have retrofitted Jet Skis and Sea-Doos to create a small army of unmanned drones to disrupt the Russian navy. And the teams of Ukrainian soldiers sent to the United States for training on Patriot missiles adapted to their new systems so quickly and completely, they were given extra, intensive training rarely offered—even to Americans.[2]

> *Throughout the Ukrainian army, this culture of team*
> *adaptiveness in a time of crisis is pervasive and hasn't only*
> *revolved around technology. For example, the teams in one*
> *Ukrainian mechanized armor brigade have adapted their tactics*
> *to essentially wear down their Russian adversaries even while*
> *using comparably older, more vulnerable personnel carriers. These*
> *teams have found that by moving their carriers forward and*
> *backward rapidly down a field while firing across the field, they*
> *can confuse the enemy's targeting.[3] Certainly not the standard*
> *procedure any armored division team would follow, but in this*
> *crisis, it is proving effective for now.*

* * *

Of course, the crisis situations that emerge during war and natural disasters are extreme in their life-threatening potential. Even looking back on the chaos that teams and their organizations initially experienced due to COVID-19 makes some other types of organizational crises, such as scandals, pale in comparison. However, our basic responses and capabilities during crises—whether events are life-threatening or livelihood-threatening—remain similar. And experts agree that crises will continue to become more complex, more virulent, more extreme, and more frequent across *all* organizational contexts. Now more than ever, these shocks will fundamentally and unexpectedly attack basic operating principles for teams. To remain effective, teams in crisis situations must be able to turn on a dime and quickly realize that their basic assumptions and principles of functioning may no longer be relevant, and to quickly shift gears accordingly. Some teams seem able to realize almost immediately that the "rules of the game" have shifted when unexpected, unusual crisis events take place, and to take appropriate actions; other teams hesitate, or take inappropriate actions after unexpected events unfold.

Our research indicates that it's not something as ethereal as luck or sudden insight that allows some teams to deal with unexpected crises; instead, our work shows that these teams engage in *key behaviors at key times* that allow them to successfully adapt from normal operations to crisis conditions "on the fly." We strongly suspect it was these types of adaptive behaviors driving the teams in Ukraine as they faced their crises and made the initial decisions to abandon existing (and slow) artillery systems, to stop waiting on (slow) delivery of expensive missiles and drones, and to stop waiting for heavier armor—in other words, to recognize that routine responses were not working and to create innovative solutions that would.

ADAPTING ON THE FLY VERSUS SETTING THE TONE

Beginning in Chapter 2, we emphasized the importance of setting the tone—ensuring that certain patterns emerge early on in a team's time together. These patterns, such as the balanced, reciprocal interaction among members of the trauma teams we studied, increase the *likelihood* of the team being able to engage in key behaviors later during critical events—behaviors like implicit coordination and reciprocity in the case of the trauma teams and flight crews. In contrast, adapting on the fly focuses even more intently on what high-performing teams do (and when and how they do it) *during* crises as unexpected events are actually unfolding and morphing around them. In other words, it's one thing to be more *likely* to engage in the right behavior, but it's another thing to actually *do* it, and to keep doing it at the *right times*.

Ways of Adapting . . . and Not

Adapting on the fly assumes, first of all, that a team has actually recognized the need to adapt in the first place. This can be a tall order, as many crises do not present themselves wrapped up in neon and tinsel with a flashing "crisis" light, immediately recognizable by everyone on the team as an event that requires immediate action. Instead, a crisis may start as a slow burn, barely perceptible, and gradually evolve into a stealthily toxic event that someone on the team finally notices.

For example, a gradual and intermittent electrical failure in a food processing plant may make a gauge reading seem incongruent with other evidence and may cause a team member to occasionally refer to a different sensor, unaware that the malfunctioning gauge is one small harbinger of a potentially critical and *gradually* emerging crisis event. Other team members working at other locations in the plant may be simultaneously engaging in similar micro-adaptations, unbeknownst to each other, simply believing that these small workarounds are keeping things on track and efficient. Because this *pattern* of small individual team member adaptations is not recognized, and the adaptations are efficient for individuals in the short term, the entire situation leads to the failure to recognize a gradually emerging critical nonroutine situation—a sensor system failure—that requires an emergency system shutdown and coordinated crisis team response, as tainted food products may have left the facility. The challenge with this type of distributed, slow-emergence crisis is that team members are generally rewarded and praised for acting independently to keep things running smoothly and using the "empowered" autonomy they've been given to do so. But as Anita Tucker and Amy Edmondson[4] point out, these empowered team members are sorely tempted to engage in first-order problem-solving that only fixes their local problem at the moment, failing to invest the time to engage in deeper second-order problem-solving that addresses the underlying system-wide causes and could prevent a crisis later.

On the other hand, some crises emerge with clear cues that team members notice practically simultaneously. When gauges for multiple systems at the food processing plant simultaneously display incongruous warning readings, it may lead team members to share information with each other and quickly determine that a central sensor processing unit has malfunctioned. Depending on the characteristics of the crisis—that is, how unexpected and unusual it is—the team may have standard operating procedures (SOPs) to manage the event. In fact, the team may have practiced using the SOPs in simulations for just this type of crisis. However, such a scenario carries its own possible pitfalls. Having and practicing SOPs can create a team version of "having a hammer and every problem looking like a nail." In other words, SOPs can become automatic go-to solutions that encourage teams to categorize crises as problems ready to be solved by the solutions available. However, what if the crisis at hand is *similar* to the SOP-solvable problem but different in subtle-yet-critical ways? Possessing SOPs with which the team feels comfortable and competent may lead team members to overlook the critical differences and persist in using the SOPs long after it would become clear to unattached outsiders that the well-practiced routines are ineffectual for the crisis taking place. And sometimes, even with irrefutable evidence of these critical differences, teams *still* cling to well-practiced routines and SOPs during acute crises, hoping that their brute-force use will cause the situation to somehow dissipate.

Force-Fitting Routines into Crisis Situations

Part of this reticence to abandon well-practiced routines may be due to an effect termed the *threat-rigidity* response.[5] According to this thinking, when we experience a threatening situation, we become rigid in our thinking and reactions, and we tend to revert to well-learned ways of thinking and behaving . . . in other words, routines. Our ability to perceive information on the periphery narrows, and we concentrate intently on the event before us. If you have ever experienced or listened to someone else describe the phenomenon of having tunnel vision during an extremely stressful situation, this may be part of a threat-rigid response.

Here is a team tunnel vision example to illustrate. Several years ago, a three-member commercial flight crew poised to land at Miami International Airport noticed that a small light indicating that their nose gear had descended and locked into place was not properly illuminated. The crew chose to divert away from the airport while they assessed this very stressful situation. As the pilots investigated, the crew became so fixated on the light and gear issue, it failed to realize that the aircraft was slowly losing altitude, and the aircraft crashed into the Everglades—even though an automated altitude alert had sounded in the cockpit.[6]

The situation was certainly stressful, and there were likely routines and protocols to help investigate that landing gear issue. In a way, we can imagine how the crew might have been drawn into a "cognitive tunneling" or fixation response. In unusual, stressful situations, teams often turn to well-practiced routines and ignore information on the edges that does not fit into those routines. And in a few stressful situations, this reaction actually works well—but only those situations that are themselves well-known and not *discontinuous* (out of the ordinary). In those stressful-but-known situations, applying the well-learned routines developed to fit similar situations actually makes sense. For example, there are well-practiced routines to follow, both for teams in the air and on the ground, if a flight crew needs to land on a runway with malfunctioning landing gear. This is obviously a very stressful, dangerous situation and doesn't happen every day, but it is a well-known situation for which routines work well.

Unfortunately, crisis situations are stressful, threatening, *and* discontinuous—that is, unusual and involve elements or combinations of elements not previously encountered. For discontinuous events like most crises, many routines—which are developed by using information from well-known past events—are simply not going to suffice. This is why we say that crises tend to make our routines *obsolete*. Similarly unfortunate is our tendency to cling to well-learned routines when we feel threatened by the crises that render these same routines obsolete. It is very unfair: Just when we need out-of-the box thinking, our natural response is to embrace well-practiced, now-obsolete routines and shut out extraneous information that could help us.

If a team comes to the realization that the current crisis does (or has evolved in order to) neutralize routines and assumptions, the team reaches a watershed moment. Letting go of routines and SOPs, especially if a team is well-practiced in using them, and walking into the creative problem-solving arena during a critical time-pressured crisis event is a difficult, out-of-the-box, mind-bending experience for many teams. When teams do succeed in letting go of routines and realize that what they are facing is uncharted crisis territory, they enter the realm of active collective sensemaking. Sensemaking involves giving meaning to and constructing an understanding of a seemingly nonsensical situation.[7] Rather than applying routines, protocols, and SOPs that are well-understood and practiced, team members involved in sensemaking share information and together fashion a collective understanding about the dynamic situation that is unfolding and its likely trajectory in the near future. Once a team has engaged in collective sensemaking and constructed a new understanding of a novel crisis situation, new plans and actions can be fashioned in response.

SO SHOULD WE JUST FORGET ABOUT ROUTINES DURING CRISES?

Taking the above to its illogical extreme, however, would have teams abandon all routines and SOPs immediately at the slightest hint of an unusual event. That would obviously not be appropriate for at least two reasons. First, teams must gather and share information about what is unfolding in order to gauge an appropriate response. Is this something for which well-practiced routines and SOPs are appropriate—which is entirely possible—or is it clear from the onset that this is a different animal? Or is the situation ambiguous, and more information is needed before the team decides? Second, crisis events may change dramatically as they emerge. An event may begin as a well-known and well-studied problem (like the landing gear issue described above), and very quickly morph into something completely unknown and unexpected. Constant information updating and adaptation is necessary—the routines that worked well early on may still need to be jettisoned later in favor of a new strategy.

One way to think about and categorize possible team responses regarding routines during crisis situations is by using a framework that ranks a team's adaptation as Type I, Type II, or Type III.[8] Type I adaptation occurs when the crisis event unfolds very gradually and sporadically, like the food processing plant example described earlier. Individual team members make small deviations from their routines in order to adjust to the event; however, over time, if these small adjustments are not communicated, they may collectively add up to an acute problem. Type II adaptation occurs when the onset of the crisis event is apparent, but it is clear what the crisis entails and which existing routines and SOPs are appropriate to enact to mitigate the situation. Type III adaptation occurs when (1) the onset of the crisis is apparent, and (2) either existing routines and SOPs prove inadequate to mitigate the situation, or it is immediately obvious that existing routines and SOPs are inappropriate to apply to the situation. In these circumstances, arriving at the second point may take some time due to the gradual morphing of the crisis, the threat-rigid reactions of the team, or both. In either case, mitigation rests upon sensemaking and creative, collaborative team problem-solving.

The point is: *The roadblocks for teams along the path toward adaptation during crises are many.* Maybe team members act too independently and don't share the information puzzle pieces, and together end up letting a smoldering crisis burn unabated. Maybe team members do realize a crisis is occurring, but they misdiagnose its nature due to their overreliance on routines and procedures. Or maybe team members realize they are dealing with a novel, critical situation, but they fail to continuously update their understanding/plans/actions as the situation changes over time.

Together with our research partners, we conducted three studies in order to understand more about how effective teams successfully adapt to unexpected critical events. In the next chapter, we describe the first two of these projects.

THE RESEARCH

As the examples of Ukrainian team adaptiveness illustrates, teams encountering a crisis situation often reach the realization that their standard practices are no longer adequate for the situation and are now obsolete. As a result, team members typically come together to brainstorm and creatively problem solve; they share the bits and pieces of information they have all collected in their unique roles, they collect more information if needed, and they collaboratively develop new solutions and approaches to face the unexpected situation facing them. For a variety of reasons, some teams are better at doing this than others, and the first two studies we describe in this section focus on identifying the team behaviors that explain *why* this is. The first study uses data from action teams and focuses on identifying key differences between low- and high-performing teams in how and when adaptive behaviors are used to navigate critical, nonroutine events. The second study takes into account that many crises keep unfolding over time; they relentlessly change and challenge teams trying to counteract and adapt to them. Consequently, in the second study, we focus on how teams successfully adapt to exactly this kind of situation. Finally, the third study takes a close look at the role of sensemaking as a real team reaches that watershed moment and adapts to the critical, nonsensical situation it faced on 9/11.

CHAPTER 6

HOW FLIGHT CREWS AND
NUCLEAR PLANT CREWS
ADAPT DURING CRISES

A S WE EMPHASIZED IN CHAPTER 5, THERE IS
quite a difference between setting the tone during a team's
first minutes together (or during its efforts to thoroughly understand the information at hand) before the team begins actively dealing with a complex situation and what it actually does on the fly while in the middle of a critical event. The first section of this book focused on the former; this section focuses on the latter.

To that end, here are two highly realistic behavioral simulation studies we have done that capture the behavioral differences between lower- and higher-performing teams as they found themselves right in the middle of crisis situations. The first study—an exploration of commercial flight crews' adaptive behaviors as they encountered unexpected critical situations—focused on pinpointing the significant differences between lower- and higher-performing crews based on what behaviors occurred and when. This was very important information for the trainers of these crews; it allowed them to fine-tune and optimize their future training resources and valuable crew training time in order to increase crew performance during critical events.

The second study—a study of nuclear power plant control room crews—again focused on identifying behavioral differences between low- and high-performing crews, but with some important changes as compared to the flight crew study. First, these crews were larger, averaging about five people rather than three. Second, the critical situations these crews faced involved more systems and therefore more varied and dynamic information for the teams to process as the crisis unfolded. And, as it turned out, a big adaptive difference in the crews indeed involved that information processing and when it occurred. How high-performing crews timed information sharing and processing differed significantly from other crews; additionally, this difference was an adaptive behavior that had not previously been empirically identified. As a result, the Institute of Nuclear Power Operations (INPO) chose to highlight this behavior in training information for U.S. nuclear plant crews.

STUDY #1: COMMERCIAL FLIGHT CREWS[1]

The Setting. This study, led by Mary, was based on video recordings of ten three-person flight crews "flying" the same leg of flight in a Boeing 727 full-motion flight simulator. The flight crews were composed of full-time commercial pilots who worked for the same major U.S. airline, and their simulator flight was part of their regularly scheduled recurrent training. Crews were composed of one captain, one first officer, and one second officer, all randomly assigned to their crews. Importantly, this simulator training was not a walk in the park for the pilots; their reputations were on the line, and if they performed badly, they could receive additional mandatory training or other negative outcomes.

The pilots had been told that they would be flying six flights in the simulator, and the video that provided data for this study was the fifth flight; in reality, the pilots only flew five flights, and had been told they would have six flights in order to decrease their anticipation that something "nasty" would be thrown at them in their last training flight. In fact, the fifth flight was their last flight, and it was indeed nasty. The simulation designers and trainers began the flight with bad weather, which complicated things, and included a route that demanded a noisy, steep descent—also difficult. But then, just as crews were ready to land, the simulation hit them with the big event: the nasty surprise of an unexpected hydraulic failure that made the nose wheel steering inoperative and necessitated cranking the landing gear down by hand. This failure also limited wing flap configuration that could be used for landing. The majority of crews quickly decided to abort their landing when all this happened by using a "go-around" procedure and proceeding to land at an alternate nearby airport.

Given this situation, and as mentioned above, the overarching goal of the study was to identify the differences in adaptation between high- and low-performing crews.

Study Design. At first blush, one might think: What can we learn from just ten teams? The answer is: It depends on how the data are collected and analyzed. Are we guessing at how teams work by looking at the outside, or are we figuratively "dissecting" them into micro-behavioral processes? We would describe the data analysis procedure for this study more as micro-behavioral dissecting.

Based on a careful analysis of existing published evidence, we identified three behaviors that are key to a team's ability to adapt to an unexpected event: information collection and transfer, task prioritization, and task distribution. *Information collection and transfer behavior* involved crew members reactively receiving information, proactively acquiring information, or sharing information with other crew members. For example, if a crew member contacted air traffic control to ask to fly at a different altitude, or if a crew member read the information on a gauge to another crew member, both behaviors would be coded as information collection and transfer. *Task prioritization behavior* involved any mentions by crew members of relative task importance, order, sequencing, or the order of task arrangement. If the captain reminded other crew members that a checklist should be run before contacting ground control, that behavior was coded as task prioritization. *Task distribution behavior* involved verbally assigning tasks to oneself or other crew members. For example, if the captain said that he would fly while the first officer computed the flaps configuration, that statement was coded as task distribution behavior.

Along with an expert independent coder, we watched each video and coded these three behaviors as present (1) or absent (0) in each *ten-second interval* of video. Additionally, *crew performance* was measured based on the number of errors the crew committed during the simulation, as measured by three expert pilots who independently watched and rated each crew's performance. We also coded the times at which a crew member vocalized the occurrence of a *nonroutine event*; for example, "Hey, we don't have nose wheel steering!" would be coded as that type of vocalization.

Imagine taking a thirty-minute video and slicing it up into ten-second intervals, and then making a record of os and 1s denoting the presence or absence of these three key adaptive behaviors within each interval, in temporal order. After the coding, each crew was represented by three strings of os and 1s, each representing one of the three key adaptive behaviors over time for that crew. In addition to tracking the presence or absence of the three behaviors over time for each crew, we also knew exactly when each crew learned of the hydraulic failure that set off the crisis during the flight. Based on the performance scores provided by the expert raters, we created two groups of crews: low- and high-performers. Our analyses focused on understanding whether or not high-performing crews adapted more than the low-performing crews—that is, did they engage in more of the three adaptive behaviors. The results, which we cover next, were surprising.

Results. When we examined the differences in the quantity of adaptive behaviors between the low- and high-performing crews, the only significant difference was information collection and transfer; high-performing crews did much more collecting and sharing of information as compared to the low-performing crews. But what about task prioritization and task distribution? We went back and rewatched the videos, and we realized that the difference wasn't just *how much* adaptive behavior was going on in these crews, but *when* it was happening. Using a statistical technique called a conditional likelihood logit model,[2] we looked for differences in the *timing* of adaptive behaviors between low- and high-performers, and we hit the bullseye. We found that high-performing crews were more than *twice as likely* as low-performing crews to prioritize tasks or distribute tasks *immediately* after the verbalization of a nonroutine event. That's how they adapted on the fly—and quickly! The lower-performing crews, if they engaged in these adaptive behaviors at all, did them much more slowly, often allowing so much time to elapse as to make the adaptive effort ineffective.

The general takeaway is that better-performing teams collect and share more information over a series of critical incidents, and specifically prioritize and distribute tasks in response to unexpected, nonroutine events. And they may cycle back through these behaviors again and again if they sense *changes* in the situation. Lower-performing teams may end up doing these things, but do them significantly slower—or maybe do only one or two of the three, or maybe none at all.

STUDY #2: NUCLEAR POWER PLANT CONTROL ROOM CREWS[3]

The Setting. While the previous study focused mainly on understanding differences between low- and high-performing teams in when and what they were doing on the fly in response to unexpected critical situations, this study, also led by Mary, took a slightly different approach. We still wanted to understand differences between low- and high-performing teams in how they adapt on the fly during nonroutine events, but we also wondered if these teams perhaps prepare for nonroutine events differently during *routine* periods of work.

The teams we collected data from for this study were fourteen four- to six-person nuclear power plant control room crews working in the same facility. Each crew consisted of a shift supervisor, control room supervisor, primary operator, secondary operator, third reactor operator (six-person crews only), and shift technical advisor (role combined with shift supervisor in four-person crews). The crews took the simulation extremely seriously, as crew members could face sanctions should their performance be rated below standards. The simulator room was a full-scale replica of the real control room for the plant, complete with working controls, lights, computer outputs, printers, and warning sounds, all connected to the simulator computer, which was programmed by the professional training staff to react to the crew's actions just as the actual plant would.

The simulation scenario included a mixture of scripted monitoring situations, routine situations, and nonroutine situations. *Monitoring situations* required crew members to be vigilant in monitoring the numerous complex systems involved in the plant, as indicated by the plethora of gauges, lights, and controls in the simulator room. *Routine situations* required crew members to recognize system cues and enact well-learned protocols. *Nonroutine situations* included problems such as a leak in the steam generator tube requiring a plant shutdown, instrumentation and power failures causing a loss of coolant requiring a plant shutdown, and a sudden loss of all feedwater to the steam generator.

Study Design. We coded data from the video recordings of the crews as they worked during their simulation, noting the presence or absence during ten-second intervals of basically the same key adaptive behaviors that we studied in the commercial flight crew research: information collection (which included verbally acquiring information on tasks, resources, deadlines, or quality of performance), task prioritization, and task distribution. But for this study, we added a new "adapt on the fly" behavior to code: *shared mental model development*. Shared mental models can be thought of as the "piece of music" that everyone is playing from—or the common knowledge or understanding that everyone is using in a situation. Without a shared mental model, crew members may go off in their own directions and actually work against each other in an uncoordinated way. Because these crews were dealing with non-routine situations that were extremely dynamic—that is, twisting, turning, and changing over time—we wanted to capture and code crew behavior that involved building and updating their shared mental models.

Lucky for us, these nuclear power plant crews made seeing when they were building their shared mental model very easy. Whenever crew members needed clarification about what was going on or what the plan for the crew was, they called out a code word: *tailboard.*[4] Then all crew members would quickly assemble at the center of the room and exchange information, update their understanding of the situation, coordinate their next actions, and disband with the words "This tailboard is concluded." At that point, crew members would return to their posts.

Finally, as with most of our previous studies of action teams, the performance of these crews was measured by multiple expert raters who, using industry-standard forms and definitions, noted the number of performance deficiencies of each crew during the simulation.[5]

Results. Based on the experts' ratings, seven crews were high performers with no observed performance deficiencies, and the other seven crews were low performers with some performance deficiencies. Our analyses surprised us in this study. The low-performing crews did *more* information collection and task prioritization—two key adaptive behaviors—than high performers overall (that is, across all three situations combined: monitoring, routine, and nonroutine). They also engaged in virtually the same amount of other key behaviors (task distribution and shared mental model development) as higher-performing crews. How could that be?

More analysis showed us what really separated the high from the low performers here, and it was very similar to the story with the flight crews: doing the
right thing *at the right time* in order to adapt on the fly. The high-performing
crews blew the other crews out of the water with information collection and
building a shared mental model *during nonroutine situations*. On top of this,
they engaged in significantly more face-to-face communication during nonroutine situations compared to the lower performers. Imagine what's happening here: As a critical situation is unfolding, the high-performing crews are
calling more face-to-face tailboards, sharing more information, updating their
shared mental models, and staying ahead of a fast-moving situation. The lower
performers are constantly engaged in a low level of sharing information and
shuffling tasks, but they spend *less* of their time during nonroutine situations
actually *adapting on the fly* with the key behaviors that would help them do so.

Practical Takeaways for Chapter 6

- Use periods of relative calm during crises to share information. Use these periods to develop
  a shared team mental model—which also may mean questioning the prevailing one.

- When feasible, interact face-to-face to share information and develop a shared mental
  model. The team leader (or any team member) should initiate briefings for this purpose. This
  should occur as standard practice, even when the crisis seems well-understood.

- During focused briefings, each member should share their understanding of what has happened, is happening, and will happen next. Ideally, members should consider these questions (and, when feasible, document their responses) before voicing their responses—to
  avoid groupthink.

- Prioritize and distribute tasks immediately upon the onset of the crisis. This is especially the
  case when the nature of the crisis and its remediation are clear and well-understood.

- Ensure members continually share information as understanding the crisis unfolds. Members should be encouraged to share their observations and task status. Teams may even institute rules such that members must provide updates when beginning and concluding certain
  tasks or at regular points in SOPs. Such sharing allows for rapid assessment of the changing scenario and, in turn, the team leader quickly reprioritizing and redistributing tasks as
  necessary.

CHAPTER 7

HOW THE NEADS TEAM ADAPTED TO THE NONSENSICAL ON 9/11

T HE FINAL RESEARCH EXAMPLE WE WILL USE here to illustrate *adapting on the fly* involves a unique study of one particular team. As evidenced by the previous chapters, we usually conduct studies of multiple teams facing the same critical situation, and then analyze their behaviors to better understand what the high-performing teams do differently as compared to the low-performing teams. And all of these teams are typically composed of highly trained professionals who take their jobs (and their simulation training) very seriously. Such studies offer excellent opportunities for us to dig deep into the behaviors of teams as they grapple with critical, complex situations.

However, sometimes it is possible to obtain data from a real team as it faces a real crisis situation. The drawback of these data is that we typically only have the opportunity to learn from one team (or very few teams). Also, the data we are able to gather are very messy since the situation was not a planned, organized study. But the great advantage of the data is that the source is a team that was truly experiencing a crisis event in real time.

The study described below focuses on a military team as it dealt with the terrorist attacks in the United States on 9/11. How this team was able to adapt on the fly and the process it followed should help convince anyone that whether they are facing a simulated or real crisis, high-performing teams are able to let go of routines, see past misinformation, and create new logics in order to understand the chaos around them.

THE NORTHEAST AIR DEFENSE SECTOR (NEADS) TEAM[1]

The Setting. On the morning of September 11, 2001, the Northeast Air Defense Sector (NEADS) organization, located in Upstate New York, included a crew of approximately thirty-six personnel who worked on the NEADS operations center floor in separate functional areas, such as the Information Section, Radar Control, Weapons Team, and Command.[2] This large team, led by a small core command team, was responsible for defending the airspace over the northeast quadrant of the United States; its primary mission was to defend the sector against external attacks, per the 9/11 Report.[3] In order to facilitate this mission, NEADS could order fighter aircraft into action, and NEADS personnel received ongoing training on protocols for responding to aircraft hijackings. On the morning of 9/11, NEADS crew members knew they were scheduled for simulated event training and were expecting something "unusual" to happen.

Study Design. For this study, led by Mary working with Dr. Sjir Uitdewilligen, we wanted to understand how the NEADS team was able to adapt on the fly and shift its initial expectation for the day (i.e., a training simulation) to be able to respond to the actual crisis situation. This shifting would involve the team being able to let go of its routines and to begin sensemaking—hypothesizing about what was really happening, as it was happening—and finally creating new action plans based on that sensemaking. Given that we were not present with the team on 9/11, we collected data from two sources: the 9/11 Commission Report transcripts, and the thirty audio recordings and transcripts shared with us by author Michael Bronner, who sourced them from NORAD (North American Aerospace Defense Command). The Bronner audio recordings captured conversations among personnel at NEADS, and between NEADS personnel and Federal Aviation Administration and other organizations' personnel on 9/11. In all, we used three transcripts from the 9/11 Commission Report and twenty-eight of the thirty Bronner transcripts in our examination of how NEADS adapted on the fly; the first two Bronner transcripts were omitted due to their non-work content.

We first coded each transcript as to the sender of the communication. Because we wanted to understand the adaptation of the NEADS team, we eliminated communication initiated by others, leaving twenty-four transcripts. Our second step in coding the remaining transcripts involved grouping the transcripts as to the working hypothesis of the speaker. It became very clear on some transcripts that the speaker's assumption was that a training exercise was taking place—in other words, everything was routine. For other transcripts, however, speakers concluded that a hijacking was taking place; this was not a routine event, but there were practiced routines and SOPs to enact for hijackings. Finally, for some transcripts, speakers voiced their confusion, fear, and concern that what was happening was a coordinated attack using commercial aircraft as missiles, and that a new, unique approach was needed.

Results. When we examined the timing of the transcripts in terms of speakers' hypotheses along with the timing of key events, such as hijacking and receiving false information, a fuller picture of how the team transitioned its understanding and adapted on the fly came into view. Some examples of statements from NEADS members shown in the following table first typified the general assumption that what was happening *must* be part of the scheduled training simulation. While some team members still held on to this assumption, others started realizing that a real hijack (and soon thereafter, multiple hijackings) was occurring. Finally, with less time overlap between the protocol hijack hypothesis, the team came to the shared realization that a coordinated attack was taking place, and they activated resources for a response.

In this real-world situation, it is possible that the NEADS team's sensemaking involved holding two working hypotheses simultaneously: a training simulation and a protocol hijacking. The entire team started the day thinking that some sort of simulation would unfold. Some members of the team may have continued to believe that a training simulation was taking place after the first and even after the second hijacking occurred; however, regardless of whether team members held either hypothesis, if the crisis had been a protocol hijacking, their routines and SOPs would have been a satisfactory adaptive response.

The wake-up call came with the third hijacking and word of crashes. This was no ordinary hijacking or even multiple hijacking. Suddenly, anyone holding

TABLE 7.   Sample of NEADS Transcript Comments

Mental Model	Time	NEADS Statements	Interpretation
Training simulation	8:37:52	Is this real-world or exercise?	Indicates that team member was using a training simulation mental model.
	8:43:06	I've never seen so much real-world stuff happen during an exercise.	
Hijack(s) fitting SOP training protocols	8:46:36	And probably right now with what's going on in the cockpit it's probably really crazy. So, it probably needs to—that will simmer down and we'll probably get some better information.	Indicates a hijack mental model with an assumption that hijackers, following past hijacking events, will later make their demands known.
	9:03:17	They have a second possible hijack!	
Coordinated attack	9:08	We need to talk to the FAA. We need to tell 'em if this stuff is gonna keep on going, we need to take those fighters, put 'em over Manhattan . . . At least we got some kind of play.	Indicates an attack mental model with a realization of multiple coordinated "hijacks" that are in all likelihood attacks.
	9:21:50	I think we need to scramble Langley [fighter jets] right now. And I'm—I'm gonna take the fighters from Otis and try to chase this guy down if I can find him.	
	9:23	These guys are smart. They knew exactly what they wanted to do.	

on to the idea that this was a simulation was quickly forced to let go of that notion. And that ability—to let go of well-learned, well-practiced routines and step into the unknown—can be completely unnerving. Any crisis situation can engender perceptions of threat, but having the rug pulled out from under us and not understanding what is happening can create what has been defined as *meaning threat*.[4] When someone experiences meaning threat, the routines and assumptions that have functioned well for them in the past are rendered obsolete, and nothing is making sense. This situation has also been referred to as a "cosmology episode" as discussed in Chapter 1.

So being stuck in meaning threat (or a cosmology episode) as we are trying to adapt on the fly to an unexpected, unusual crisis situation is definitely something we want to avoid. But how? How did the NEADS team manage to go from thinking it was dealing with a training simulation to adapting to multiple hijacks to reaching the realization that terrorists were attacking with commercial aircraft—in the space of approximately thirty minutes? One learning point we can derive from NEADS, and that others have written about as well, is the nonlinear trajectory of team adaptation. The NEADS team members held multiple hypotheses at the same time, and yet coordinated their information sharing and responses. They did not move in lockstep, en masse from hypothesis to hypothesis; instead, they shared different opinions and information in a free-ranging, collective sensemaking effort that was geared toward one thing: understanding their context at the moment. That is a learned team skill that not all teams possess, but it is absolutely necessary for adapting on the fly when the critical event is something never before encountered. And what types of teams are likely to possess this skill? Teams with high levels of psychological safety, reciprocity (remember communication balance from Part I on setting the tone?), and respect. These may seem like group hug, ethereal concepts, but even for military teams, they make a difference when it really counts.

We also include an "Adapting on the Fly Checklist" at the end of this section. This checklist is based on the material from Chapters 6 and 7. It is a practical tool that teams can use mid-crisis, but we also encourage using it in training simulations. We emphasize the importance of doing so because some of the prescriptions we offer here will feel unnatural for many teams. For instance, holding—let alone encouraging—multiple hypotheses about an ongoing event, versus jumping to a conclusion, is just not the norm for most teams. When multiple hypotheses are mentioned, they often reflect members' attempts to "be the right one"—as in the solution competition we described in Chapter 4. Furthermore, considering multiple ideas at the same time requires skill; team members must figure out how to keep the different hypotheses "in mind" and evaluate incoming information against them each. These norms and skills can be developed in simulation training, as we elaborate upon in Chapter 13, such that team members do not need to think about how to implement them when crises strike; they have become automatic. In contrast, trying to implement them for the first time during the actual crisis, absent practice, is a bit like going on the stage without a rehearsal; it perhaps may go okay, but who wants to take that risk?

TABLE 8.   Adapting on the Fly Checklist

Y or N	Behavioral Marker	Interpretation
	All team members share their relevant information about the crisis and their interpretation of it. This occurs prior to discussions about strategies to address the crisis.	**Y** = Members have ample time and psychological safety to share information about the crisis. *If N...* • *Regularly ask each team member to provide information. What are they noticing that looks out of place? What are they seeing or hearing that other team members should know?* • *Consider asking each team member to provide X pieces of information during each team briefing.* • *Train the team so that nobody can offer solutions before everyone has provided X pieces of information or perhaps even until a certain amount of time has elapsed in the simulation training.*
	Tasks are prioritized and roles are distributed immediately (after the onset of the crisis and when it shifts in significant ways).	**Y** = Team members have shared information. This allows for distinct pieces of information to be connected → patterns to be detected → the team to adapt. This also signals that the team (leader) appreciates the necessity of adapting to address the crisis immediately. *If N...* • *Team members independently consider "worst-case scenarios" given the known information. In developing scenarios, team members may depict specifically what would happen . . . and when. This exercise can help the team discover possible downstream outcomes of not acting sooner (i.e., the potential value of adapting immediately).* • *Act! If nobody else steps up to prioritize tasks and distribute roles, do so! Do not wait for a formal leader. Psychological evidence indicates that people respond to direct requests more than one might think.*

	During periods of relative calm downtime during a crisis, the team is meeting to update its shared mental model and discuss contingencies and next steps.	**Y** = Team members are sharing information about what they have observed, generating hypotheses about the crisis, and comparing that information against the multiple hypotheses.
		
		If N...
		• *Train teams that these periods of "downtime" are when much of the strategizing happens. During a crisis, the team leader (or other members) need to initiate the whole-team briefings and/or interactions with individual members.*
		• *The team leader needs to ask:*
		  o *"What do you think is happening here?" etc. If feasible, ask members separately before the team as a whole to avoid groupthink.*
		  o *"What else could be happening? What possibilities are we missing?"*
		  o *"What is each of you doing now, going forward?"*
		  o *"What will we do if X happens? If Y happens?"*
		  (continued)

TABLE 8.   (*continued*)

Y or N	Behavioral Marker	Interpretation
	Team members regularly update each other with information about the crisis as it unfolds.	**Y** = Team members are scanning the environment; they recognize what information may be useful to others on the team. *If N . . .* • *Directly ask each team member to share what other team members need to know. You could do this at regular intervals, but it ideally should happen organically, when a team member encounters/learns that information. Emphasize that, for the remainder of the crisis, team members need to share information they believe may be useful to others without being asked for it. Use closed-loop communication.* • *During simulation training, have team members privately list every piece of information they believe may be useful to others in specific roles. They also should list what information would be useful for them to have. Then, have the team members share lists. This will help members learn what needs to be shared.* • *Use cross-role training. Have members take on each other's roles during simulation training. Even if they cannot perform all technical tasks, they will get a sense of what that person's tasks are like and what information that person needs to know during a crisis.*

Practical Takeaways for Chapter 7

- Generate multiple hypotheses about the nature of the crisis. Resist the tendency to make definitive conclusions about what is transpiring.

- (Encourage team members to) regularly question whether the current hypothesis fits the observations. When your team institutes a procedure, resist allowing the steps of that procedure to dictate understanding of the crisis. Continue to monitor the broader context for alternative explanations and additional information.

- Ensure a psychologically safe environment for team members to "poke holes" in current understandings of the crisis and to propose others that are "outside the box."

- Treat sensemaking as an ongoing, dialectical process. Team sensemaking entails members continually sharing their observations about what is occurring and then assembling those data points to generate and test understandings about the crisis.

PART III

FINDING THE BALANCE

What Are the Three Key Tensions That Successful Team Leaders Manage in Their Teams during a Crisis?

CHAPTER 8

TEAM LEADERS
AND TENSIONS

*Captain Al Haynes, First Officer Bill Records, and Second
Officer Dudley Dvorak were flying United Airlines Flight 232
over Iowa from Denver to Chicago, cruising at 37,000 feet
on autopilot, when the number two (tail-mounted) engine
disintegrated after a loud explosion. One engine on each wing
remained. Fourteen seconds later, Records said, "Al, I can't
control the airplane." Dvorak read the routine protocol checklist
for shutting down number two engine. The first item was "close
the throttle." But the throttle would not close. The second item
was to close off the fuel supply to the engine, but the fuel lever
would not move. Then Dudley said to actuate the firewall
shut-off valve. When Al Haynes did that, the fuel supply to the
engine was finally shut off.*

*As the out-of-control aircraft began to roll upside down—which
would have been an unrecoverable situation—Al Haynes
slammed the engine number one throttle closed and firewalled
the number three throttle, and the right wing came slowly back
level. Haynes was later asked how the crew thought to use the
differential thrust of the two surviving wing-mounted engines to*

control the aircraft. He answered: "I do not have the foggiest idea. There was nothing left to do, I guess, but it worked."

After fifteen minutes, the flight crew was advised that Captain Dennis Fitch was a passenger in first class, and Fitch was invited to the flight deck. For the next thirty minutes, Fitch operated the one and three throttle levers, keeping the aircraft moderately level while they approached Sioux City. Correcting the aircraft altitude by using the throttles of the existing two engines was an entirely new aircraft handling technique, and the subsequent maneuvering techniques used by other crew members to navigate and land were also entirely novel. As a result of the crew's efforts, 184 of the 296 people aboard UA232 survived a crash for which the National Transportation Safety Board (NTSB) concluded a safe landing had been virtually impossible. The NTSB also stated that "under the circumstances the UAL [United Airlines] flight crew performance was highly commendable and greatly exceeded reasonable expectations."

The more than one hundred years of combined flying experience on the flight deck were skillfully exploited by Al Haynes's use of crew resource management techniques. But neither prior experience nor new techniques seem to be the defining features of heroic recovery; both can be involved, and the appropriate balance *depends very largely upon those involved and the nature of the emergency situation. These preponderances have to be* finely tuned *to the needs of the prevailing circumstances.*[1]

* * *

Faced with an unexpected crisis, Captain Al Haynes and his crew certainly were able to adapt on the fly—using the abilities we discussed in Chapters 5, 6, and 7. They collected information from the systems on the aircraft and from air traffic control; furthermore, they reprioritized their tasks and real-located themselves quickly across those tasks again and again as the situation unfolded. They shared ideas and coordinated, constantly checking in with each other and updating their understanding of a situation none of them had ever encountered. And they stepped in and backed each other up, calling out information and even judiciously using humor on occasion.

But this exceptional crew was somehow able, over the course of the extraordinary crisis, to *maintain* its focus and effectiveness throughout a *series* of roiling, emergent, unpredictable events. How? As noted in our opening vignette, this crew managed to achieve the perfect *balance* of relying just enough on experience and deep knowledge of operating procedures while also making plenty of room for experimentation and creative thought. Sensing, monitoring, and managing this balance—this *tension*, if you will—between *established knowledge* and *routines* versus *creativity and improvisation* is something our research suggests is critically important during an unexpected, nonroutine situation. In fact, one of the most important functions for the leader during a critical event is to engage in team-level *metacognition*: stepping back periodically to assess how the team is thinking and problem-solving, and adjusting the balance between three key *tensions* that we have identified in our research. In this chapter, we will dig into what these tensions are and how team leaders and team members can successfully maintain this balance.

Of the key team behavior concepts covered in this book, finding the balance is probably the most difficult to achieve. This difficulty stems from three factors. First, just as objects tend to stay in motion or at rest, teams tend to become fixed in how they are responding to a critical event. A team responding to an event by using a checklist will tend to continue progressing through the checklist. In contrast, a team that decides to abandon the checklist and act spontaneously is unlikely to bring out the checklist later. Sometimes sticking to one approach is efficient and productive; other times, particularly in dynamic and unpredictable situations, switching to another approach is necessary.

A second reason achieving balance is difficult has to do with the *timing*. Balance is not just about teams shifting approaches over the course of the crisis, nor is it about aiming for a "magic" ratio or overall proportion of how much time teams should spend doing one thing versus others. Effective balancing is about knowing *when* the team should shift. You might think about this in terms of the idea of work and non-work activity. While most of us strive to find some balance between working and non-work activities, "good balance" implicitly means *more* than just finding the "right" ratio of time spent in each. It means knowing *when* to do work and when not to. For example, if you know during which part of the day you are most productive or at which phase of team projects your contribution would matter most, you know *when* to work—not just how much. Of course, knowing when to do what is not always easy—especially when the situation is unclear and a group of people may have different opinions about how to proceed. So, while the first difficulty is about the tendency to continue in one approach, this second challenge is about knowing when to shift from one approach to another.

Achieving balance is difficult for a third reason too: Balance requires the *metacognition* mentioned above. Metacognition is an extremely important psychological concept for individual learning and performance across various domains. For teams, metacognition is about being able to see the bigger picture and to reflect on questions like, "What is happening?" "Are our strategies working?" "What are we missing here?" Taking this bird's-eye view to address these larger questions enables teams to achieve balance. It lets the team see when it needs to switch between planning versus initiating that plan, for example, and when the team needs to speed up or slow down. And any member of the team—not just a formal leader—can perform and share ideas rooted in metacognition. We will explore the importance of metacognition for achieving balance in the following pages.

THE THREE TENSIONS TEAMS FACE DURING CRISIS EVENTS

As mentioned above, we have identified three key tensions that teams need to balance during crises in our research. We first describe these tensions and then discuss three studies, one demonstrating how teams effectively balance each respective tension. **Routine versus Improvisation.** One tension crisis teams must balance is operating in a *routine, procedural manner* versus acting in a more *improvisational manner.*[2]

Imagine a team learns it soon will be addressing an unexpected, critical problem. The team has some information about the problem, but the information is incomplete. Thus, the team knows it is facing a crisis but is unsure of all the facts associated with it or how best to address it. This could be a trauma team preparing to treat a patient just brought in from an auto collision, a SWAT team arriving at a hostage situation, or the public relations team of a large development company learning that one of their structures just collapsed and injured several people. In each of these cases, teams act by trying to gather information about the event while—often concurrently—implementing actions meant to contain it and/or mitigate the event's reverberations.

The well-prepared team already has established protocols for how to respond to a "known" crisis situation. The SWAT team, for example, has formal procedural ways of responding in a hostage situation. So too do teams like those we have studied in aviation, nuclear power, and similar settings. For other types of teams, there may not be a documented procedure per se, but teams still follow an internal script. If the current situation looks similar to previous ones, the team responds with the same set of behaviors it has used in the past or that team members have used with other teams in the past. This is not necessarily explicitly discussed or even consciously recognized among team members. The series of steps the team follows can unfold somewhat automatically.

This routinized response is not only apparent in the actions that teams execute in trying to quell the crisis; it also is key in how the team members interact with each other during the execution of those actions. Sometimes, this routinization is dictated, such as in formal protocols or chains of command. In teams with very clear hierarchies, each member knows exactly with whom to communicate, about what, and when. Often, though, these communication dynamics are not explicit; they come from past experience and a general sense of "how we communicate around here." Thus, for example, in a team in which the leader usually calls the meetings and does most of the talking during those meetings, the rest of the team likely expects the same pattern to emerge during a crisis.

Whether through formal training and procedures or the result of experience and preconceived expectations, acting in routine, standardized ways is a common team response to crises. As we discussed in an earlier chapter, crises are threatening experiences for most people, and under threat, we tend to rely on using well-learned, well-practiced behaviors; this principle is, as we previously described, a well-known concept called the "threat-rigidity" hypothesis.[3] And, on one hand, there obviously are many benefits to being consistent and following such routines. Routines provide structure and coordination. They also reduce uncertainty and distress for team members in what is already an uncertain and distressing environment. Members know their roles and prescribed actions; they do not need to negotiate them when the crisis begins.

Also, when interacting, team members do not have to deliberate about what they should say to whom, and when; this all is well-established—even if individuals are not consciously aware of these underlying social dynamics.

On the other hand, following these routines is not always beneficial. Sometimes, deviating from routine and instead improvising is necessary. The importance of improvisation was evident in the opening vignette of the chapter, when the flight crew had to abandon many routines and experiment. This was a novel set of circumstances, necessitating such improvisation. In other cases, routines can act as "blinders" of sorts. We have seen many cases in which teams become so focused on adhering to team norms or carrying out a prescribed set of actions that they fail to notice that another, more pressing problem has emerged and/or that the actions they have chosen to implement are not actually solving the root problem.

Again, though, following routine or not sometimes is just as important in terms of *how* team members interact during the crisis as it is for *what actions* the team executes. In fact, deviating from established team communication patterns can sometimes offset problems caused by sticking to or not sticking to routines. As an example of this interplay, consider the case of United Airlines Flight 173, which crash-landed in Oregon in December of 1978, killing ten on board. The plane crashed because its low fuel state led to engine fuel exhaustion. Among the notable facts about this incident is that the crew did not, in fact, adhere to some routine procedures that otherwise may have *prevented* the crash. The crew was fixated on diagnosing a landing gear problem—a *nonroutine* event—but neglected the *routine* monitoring of fuel. Perhaps even more notable, though, is that the two other crew members alerted the pilot to the low fuel level, but they did not do so assertively enough to capture his attention. Had they deviated from this particular communication norm, more strongly asserting themselves (at a time when doing so was not emphasized as much in aviation training as it is today), the copilots perhaps could have prevented the crash.

As this example makes clear, there are times when teams also must diverge from acting in a consistent and standardized manner, and when improvisation becomes necessary. Obviously, though, teams typically still need some routine and structure. The idea of a flight crew, firefighting crew, or top management team responding to a crisis in a completely unstructured manner is an absurd one. Teams need some level of protocol, routine, and consistency. Thus, the critical question would seem to be that of *when and how* do teams strike this *balance* of adhering to routine and consistency versus improvisation and change over time during a crisis. This is the question we explore in Chapter 9.

Planning versus Acting. A second type of balance teams must manage over time during a crisis is that between *planning and acting.* When faced with crises, teams need to implement restorative procedures and do so quickly. A matter of a minute or less can mean all the difference in contexts like a hospital trauma bay. However, teams also need to plan what they are going to do. The team may have only one opportunity to act before the situation becomes a categorically different one to address or before the situation deteriorates beyond repair (e.g., as with trauma patients). Choosing the wrong actions or implementing the correct actions poorly can mean the missed opportunity to save a life, prevent a highly publicized scandal, and so on. Thus, the team must find the right balance in terms of planning and acting; doing too much of either, without the other, could be costly.

Beyond just finding the right balance, though, the team also must decide *when* to plan or act. First, at the beginning of the crisis, the team needs to decide how much strategizing is "enough." The team must determine when the "ax is sharp enough," weighing the seriousness and time pressure of the scenario against the likely success of their plan and the potential added benefit of spending more time developing that plan. For example, authorities have criticized the police's decision to wait nearly eighty minutes, ostensibly planning and deciding to wait on the arrival of extra armor, before entering the schoolroom where an active shooter tragically killed nineteen schoolchildren and two adults in Uvalde, Texas. Whether this decision ultimately was the wrong one or not is not conclusively known at this time, but the fact that it is under scrutiny illustrates this tension.

Beyond making an initial decision, though, the team repeatedly must choose when it has time to assess, and strategize about, the actions it is currently implementing—along with the evolving crisis those actions are intended to address. Because crises change in unpredictable and often nonlinear ways, and because their underlying causes frequently remain obscured, teams must plan "in-process," as the crisis unfolds and the team attempts to combat it.

Thus, the team needs to determine *when* to plan, despite having to concurrently address the crisis, and when to stop planning and return to full action.

Of course, these questions of how to strike this balance and when to transition are not specific to crises. Project teams of all kinds need to make these judgment calls. One needs to be certain enough that a plan will work, yet avoid so-called "analysis paralysis." Indeed, other research has established that teams tend to cycle between "action" and "transition" phases.[4] Action phases refer to when teams engage and execute important tasks. Between these action phases are periods of non-action transition phases. It is during these transition phases that teams reflect, plan, and strategize. For example, a marketing team may have periods of intense action, such as in the days leading up to sending a new advertising campaign to a client. At some point after that, though, it likely will have some window of time to reflect on its team processes and strategize about next steps.

Two aspects of this normal transitioning, though, look different for crisis teams. First, the temporal landscape of task activity generally looks quite discrepant for teams responding to crisis events versus for other teams. Rather than having periods of downtime without immediately pressing tasks, crisis teams are generally always executing tasks during the event. These teams typically do not have the luxury of prolonged strategy sessions. The situations in which they operate necessitate continual work.

The second factor that makes knowing when to transition especially difficult for these teams is the attentional narrowing and compromised situational awareness that crises often breed. When the team is in the trenches, trying to address the crisis, members face stress, cognitive overload, and the challenge of managing constant communication. Collectively, these forces foster the "tunnel vision" or attentional narrowing that we described in Chapter 5. For this reason, many types of teams have a designated member whose main job is to maintain the team's metacognition and aid them in knowing when to switch from planning to execution and back again. This individual is removed from the immediate scenario—both physically and in terms of not executing any team activities/tasks. In trauma settings, this is an experienced physician who stands behind a line drawn on the floor, overseeing the physician tending to the patient and the other team members (e.g., nurses, technicians, other physicians). In nuclear power plant control room crews, the shift manager plays a similar role. Even with this arrangement, though (and certainly without it), figuring out when to plan versus act is a challenge. As we will discuss in Chapter 10, achieving the right balance between planning and acting is important for teams to successfully handle crises.

Speed versus Precision. The third type of balance often critical to teams facing crisis situations is the balance between *speed and precision*. As we previously discussed, time pressure and the need to act quickly are defining elements of crises. Firefighters know this lesson well; with each second elapsed, victims trapped inside are taking in more smoke and are at increased chances of being injured in a structural collapse. Similarly, the navy uses time as a key metric in training crews to extinguish on-ship fires. In active shooter situations, the first few minutes are usually the most crucial. In healthcare, teams are trained to reduce time until interventions (e.g., drug administration, intubation), which is related to patient outcomes. Indeed, hospitals report and benchmark these times, and are often evaluated on their average times. Public relations teams also know the importance of fast action when handling an organizational crisis; the first few hours are critical for creating and disseminating messaging on social media platforms, and determine in large part how the public will perceive the event and where they will place blame.

Obviously, acting quickly comes with its own perils, though. Trying to behave faster than we normally do generally means being less precise and more prone to error, such as in the solution fixation trap we discussed earlier. The more complex the task, the more problematic going fast will be. People make more mistakes when they try to type quickly or push their bounds when playing a musical instrument, for example, because these are activities that are simultaneously cognitively and physically demanding.

In some scenarios, we are comfortable doing things quickly because precision is not very important. Typing too quickly will produce more errors, but they can be fixed easily. In other cases, though, precision is essential. The city transit authority team that provides a press release about a bus crash and then later learns the release contained faulty information will create more harm than good for the transit authority's image. Similarly, the trauma team that examines the patient too quickly and misses assessing or reassessing a key vital sign may be setting the patient (and itself) up for a very bad outcome.

For teams facing crises, this seeming speed-precision tradeoff is a key tension. It is related to the balance of planning versus acting. But here, we are referring to the granular communication dynamics teams must manage during the height of a crisis. Instead of asking *when* or *how much* successful teams plan, the question here is: *How* do successful teams communicate and coordinate their actions to effectively handle this speed-precision tradeoff? What kinds of communication do they exchange that enable them to achieve precision and which ones are they willing to sacrifice for the sake of reducing overall time to crisis resolution?

Again, this tension exists for many types of teams, but it looks very different for teams facing crises. For the latter, *any* verbalization might detract from the essential actions team members are taking to combat the crisis (e.g., flying the aircraft during a hydraulic failure, or securing a severely wounded hiker in a basket for the helicopter to airlift). This is because both delivering and interpreting verbal communications demand cognitive resources. Thus, the person sending and the person receiving the message both have fewer resources remaining for concentrating on their primary task. If you have tried having an intense conversation while also texting someone else, you understand this idea of divided or compromised resources. You are likely to make errors in one of the conversations, or both. This fact that communicating comprises our ability to multitask is also the reason why talking on one's phone while driving is dangerous whether or not it is "hands-free"; it is not only holding the phone but talking and listening that draw away our cognitive resources.

Sometimes, teams have ample time; in these cases, teammates can ask for clarification or for team members to repeat a message; also, someone with an important message could deliver it to each team member individually, so as to ensure that person is attending. The messenger also can repeat information not received or instructions not followed.[5] But, teams operating during crises do not have these affordances. Because of the extreme time pressure they are operating under, team members must consider decisions such as: "Should I speak or not speak?"; "Should I provide more detail or the minimum detail?"; "Do I speak to the whole team or just the leader?"

Seen in this way, members need to be judicious about what to communicate and how to communicate it. Here, the maxim of "more communication is better" certainly will not always hold. Communication may create a burden, impairing execution of fundamental tasks that members must complete. And yet, crises require at least some communication, despite the time and attentional resources that it consumes.

How do effective teams manage this tension between speed and precision? A recent example of this tension comes from the search and rescue efforts from the tragic collapse of the Champlain Towers South condominium near Miami, Florida. More than eighty rescue teams initially responded to the pancake collapse, with many more coming to the scene in later days. These teams obviously needed to act with haste to try and find and rescue potential trapped victims. But they also needed to be precise in searching for the victims, avoiding further harm with their machinery, and navigating parts of the structure susceptible to further collapse. Implicit in these decisions are calculations of risk. What are the risks of moving more slowly with more precision versus moving quickly with more abandon? These are not easy calculations to make, as we discuss in Chapter 11.

THE RESEARCH

In the three chapters that follow, we describe studies that we and colleagues have conducted illustrating this idea of team balance and showing its importance for successful crisis resolution. Each chapter covers a study that illustrates balancing one of the tension types we described above. Chapter 9 describes a study that examines nuclear power plant control room crews and shows how teams can effectively manage the tension between routinization and improvisation. Chapter 10 focuses on research investigating balance in terms of planning versus action among aviation crews. Finally, Chapter 11 describes research detailing how different underground mine rescue teams navigate the precision-versus-speed tradeoff.

These three crisis contexts vary in fundamental ways. The teams are operating in vastly different physical environments, face different demands, are at varying levels of personal danger themselves in their high-fidelity simulated environments, and need to make different kinds of decisions and take distinctive actions. Despite these (and many other) differences, they all face fundamental tensions that they must balance in addressing their respective crises.

CHAPTER 9

HOW NUCLEAR PLANT CREWS BALANCE ROUTINE AND IMPROVISATION

A S WE MENTIONED IN CHAPTER 8, FINDING the balance in the three tensions we outlined—routine versus improvisation, planning versus acting, and speed versus precision—is the most complex area we've identified in our research on what separates the higher- from the lower-performing teams during crisis situations. And perhaps most vexing for some of the teams we've seen is the topic of this chapter: finding the balance between using routines versus improvisation.

Countless teams in organizations take their professional training and duties extremely seriously, and with good reason: If these teams fail to execute their tasks with precision, the results could damage not only the organization, but also the surrounding community. Think of the teams that monitor cybersecurity, or the teams that keep electrical grids up and running, or teams that monitor and maintain smooth and safe operations in large chemical plants. These teams are trained and rewarded for knowing how to enact well-trained and tested routines with precision, since the last thing anyone wants is a rogue team suddenly deciding on its own to run a chemical plant using a new, unproven method.

And yet, we know it is impossible to create enough routines to anticipate every possible unexpected critical event that may occur. Thus, the most high-performing variants of these teams are those that see where a crisis over-laps with existing routines and where it does not, rather than trying to force fit the entire crisis comfortably into their routine repertoire. In other words, these teams avoid what psychologists term "functional fixedness"[1]—or the ten-dency to apply a well-learned solution to every problem one sees (like having a hammer and seeing every problem as a nail). These teams balance the use of routines with flexibility and an ability to improvise where needed, achieving a more accurate crisis response—and stretching their own capabilities at the same time. In the study we describe next, we saw just these types of differences in the control crews of a nuclear power plant as they faced a critical situation in a highly-realistic training simulation.

STUDY #1: NUCLEAR POWER PLANT CONTROL ROOM CREWS[2]

The Setting. We conducted this study, led by Seth, at a nuclear power plant (NPP) located on the East Coast of the United States. Similar to the study described in Chapter 6, this sample of teams consisted of nuclear power plant control room operator teams engaging in semiannual simulation train-ing. The teams were permanent, meaning the operators were part of stand-ing teams who worked together regularly in the plant. Following the 1979 Three Mile Island partial meltdown incident, simulation training has become standard for NPP operators. In addition to serving training purposes, the use of high-fidelity simulations is involved in the licensing process for NPP operators—both new and experienced ones.

Given these factors, NPP operators and teams take their simulation training quite seriously. We have been struck by the gravity with which these teams ap-proach simulation-based training. In our observation, these teams universally regard these simulations as opportunities to learn and are highly invested in their team crisis performance and its evaluation.

The simulation training took place in a replica control room that was de-signed to look identical to the actual control room in which the team normally operated. This particular nuclear power plant had two operating units (i.e., reactors). Since each of the teams worked at one of the two units, they also had separate simulation rooms.

In this study, we were interested in how teams managed the tension between operating according to routine versus improvising during a crisis scenario.

Specifically, we wanted to know what kinds of team interaction patterns were associated with superior team performance during a crisis.

Owing to formal training, their past experiences (e.g., many operators in the current sample had served on nuclear submarines), and to the norms they have developed (see Chapter 1), teams often acquire routinized ways of communicating during a crisis. In our experience, though, this structured interaction pattern is not universal. Rather, we had observed that teams varied dramatically in their interaction styles when responding to emergencies. We had a hunch that these differences were linked to how well the teams performed in addressing the crisis, and so we conducted this study to investigate this question more closely.

Over the years, we had noticed that some teams indeed do seem to adhere to routinized, consistent patterns of interaction and communication throughout the duration of the crisis. What struck us as especially interesting was that this pattern of interaction always also looked very similar—irrespective of what type of team we were studying. First, these teams seemed to meet at regular intervals. These meetings or briefings were dictated either by clock time (e.g., "We'll meet again in five minutes") or by the checklist or procedure the team was using (e.g., "We have executed a series of steps; it's time to meet and discuss what's going on"). It was as if these briefings "had to take place then," regardless of the changing nature of the crisis. Even these meetings seemed to follow a set pattern of interaction. The team leader almost invariably was the person initiating the team meetings. The leader also was the person who would speak first and speak most often. When the leader solicited input from other team members, this too often happened in a systematic and uniform fashion.

Certainly, interacting in a procedural and consistent manner like this would seem to have some clear benefits. Knowing what to expect in terms of team communication plausibly frees up team members' cognitive resources, allowing them to focus on technical tasks. It also may help with coordination. If team members know who will speak, when, and in which particular ways (e.g., by providing information versus asking questions), teams should be able to establish shared mental models, thereby alleviating the costs of continuously having to negotiate and recognize changing interaction dynamics.

At the same time, adhering to this approach, even if procedure dictates it, also likely has some disadvantages. While teams benefit from having communication norms (see Chapter 2), they also would seem to benefit from improvising as the scenario changes. Indeed, we had observed that some teams interacted in less consistent and more fluid ways over the crisis lifespan. For example, we noted that some teams met at irregular intervals, seemingly as dictated by what was happening around them and their perceived capability to address the crisis—not by clock time or as a step in a procedure. A team might meet three times over two minutes and then not meet again for another ten minutes. It was not that these latter teams were interacting in chaotic or random ways; it all appeared rather calculated to us. But we wanted to understand this calculation better, unpackaging exactly *how* these latter teams improvised. We also wanted to know which approach was more effective in combating the crisis—the consistent, procedural approach, or the less consistent, improvisational one.

Study Design. We studied fourteen nuclear control room teams (i.e., crews) as they engaged in responding to simulated crises. Each crew was composed of at least three operators—one unit supervisor and two board operators. The unit supervisor is the crew leader and coordinates the actions of the other team members. The supervisor decides which procedure to implement and then guides the team as they progress through the steps outlined in that procedure. Each team also had a "left" board operator and "right" board operator (positioned on the right or left side), responsible for monitoring and controlling the reactor core, cooling systems, and emergency systems. Some teams also had additional crew members. In addition, there was a shift manager. This individual oversaw the entire control room and transpiring dynamics "at a distance"—both literally and figuratively. In general, the shift manager mainly communicated with the unit supervisor, not the board operators. When necessary, the shift manager also spoke on the phone with external stakeholders (e.g., trainers acting as representatives from the Nuclear Regulatory Commission).

Expert trainers at the plant had developed scripts of the crises to which the teams would be responding. The trainers developed these scripts by borrowing from actual incidents that had occurred at this plant or other plants. During the simulation, trainers sit in a room adjacent to the replica control room and electronically initiate the incidents in the script at specific times—for example, initiating a closed steam valve warning four minutes into the simulation.

To our advantage, these simulators already were equipped with four digital video cameras that also captured audio, arranged throughout the control rooms. This made data collection much easier for us; the data were already being collected for training purposes by the organization. After the simulation, the trainers would lead a debriefing session, sometimes referring to the recordings. This is best practice, and the nuclear power industry has been ahead of the curve on safety training for some time.

We used the recordings to code specific verbal and nonverbal actions that team members expressed as the crisis unfolded. We focused on the fifteen minutes following the onset of the crisis—as triggered by the trainers. Eleven verbal and nonverbal behaviors were coded. The coding list looked similar to those we have used in other studies. Most behaviors were verbal utterances (for example, "providing information," "providing command," "begins procedure"), and we also coded some nonverbal behaviors, such as when the crew began and ended a briefing; these are huddles someone on the team initiates to help create a shared mental model of the crisis and the next steps the crew will be executing.

Results. We wanted to determine how effective teams manage the tension between communicating in a more consistent, procedural manner versus in a more improvisational and organic one. Our primary metric of crew performance was a measure called the *anticipation ratio*. Other team researchers developed this metric to gauge team implicit coordination and shared situational awareness.[3] We calculated the anticipation ratio as follows:

$$\text{Anticipation Ratio in this Study} =$$
$$\frac{\# \textit{ of information requests voluntarily provided without solicitation}}{\# \textit{ of information requests + communication errors}}$$

Higher ratios suggest more implicit coordination and shared situational awareness, as team members are foreseeing and proactively "pushing" information—before it is requested.

The anticipation ratio is a very useful index; it is intuitive, easy to calculate, and correlated with other metrics of team communication and coordination. But it arguably is also more a measure of team process than team effectiveness. Thus, we supplemented it with a secondary measure of team performance. We asked supervisors to rate their crew's performance using a twenty-one-point scale. Fortunately, the two indices were strongly correlated, bolstering our confidence in using the anticipation ratio measure for effectiveness (i.e., performance). Using their anticipation ratio, we classified teams as either high performers or average performers.

To explore how teams managed the tension between routine versus improvisation, we examined their patterns of interaction during the crisis. Using the Theme algorithm (www.patternvision.com), we submitted the eleven coded behaviors to the pattern detection software. We then examined whether the patterns of the high performers looked different from those of the average-performing crews.

The results were clear. Members of the higher-performing crews interacted in very different ways than did those in their average-performing counterparts. First, the Theme algorithm detected fewer recurring patterns for the more effective crews than for the average crews. This means that crews who handled the crisis better did so by changing how they interacted as the nature and demands of the scenario changed—that is, they improvised and adapted as the situation evolved. In contrast, the other crews tended to maintain the same routinized pattern of communication regardless of what was happening around them.

Consistent with our hunch, this routinization—and lack of improvisation— was especially obvious in how the less successful teams handled their team meetings (i.e., briefings). As we had seen in other contexts, these crews would meet at regular intervals. Moreover, during these briefings, the crew seemed to communicate in a rather standard way; each member would speak in turn, and there was consistency in who provided what kind of information to whom.

The more successful crews interacted quite differently. Specifically, the algorithm results indicated that interactions in these crews generally involved fewer crew members. Rather than the whole crew meeting up at regular intervals, two or three crew members would speak to each other. Of course, these were not always the same people; different members communicated as the situation necessitated. Also, these smaller interactions involved fewer utterances and fewer back-and-forths in who was speaking. People interjected a brief remark to a fellow teammate when they had information to convey—even when no formal team meeting was taking place. The communication was efficient, short, and to the point. Overall, there was more of a staccato rhythm to their communication: communicate, act, communicate, act . . . and so on.

Importantly, it was not that the better performing crews talked *more* or shared more information than the other crews. In fact, the total number of communications between the two sets of teams was quite similar. As we have found elsewhere, the *patterns* of communication distinguished more versus less successful crisis teams better than the *amount* of communication does. Also, there was no difference in the number of formal procedures the two sets of crews implemented. It was not that the more effective crews invoked more (or fewer) procedures to address the crisis. What set apart the more effective crews was *how* they interacted, not that they used more or less routine in terms of the number of formal protocols implemented.

Overall, these findings show the importance of teams *being flexible* and of *striking a balance between adherence to procedure and flexibility*. Successful teams did follow routine and did enact standard operating procedures. They were far from chaotic in how they behaved. Rather, their flexibility and ability to improvise when enacting those procedures was what yielded better team outcomes. Because people shared information with (only) the particular others who needed it, and did so when they needed it, the team was able to maintain better situational awareness of the changing scenario. Crew members did not need to wait for a regularly scheduled briefing or a certain step in the procedure to communicate their readings or information; they alerted others to that information *before* others even requested it (as indicated by their higher anticipation ratio). Thus, if the team did need to pivot to a different procedure, they would know to do so sooner. In the next study, we examined a different kind of tension, that between planning and acting. In that study, we explore how teams shift between two sets of behaviors to manage this tension.

Practical Takeaways for Chapter 9

- During a crisis, ensure that members are regularly providing information to those who need it—ideally *before* they need it.
- Information exchanges do NOT have to involve all team members. Most information exchanges likely will involve subsets of team members.
- Ensure that members do NOT wait for full-team briefings to share information (e.g., what they are seeing or working on, information other team members need for their respective tasks).
- Full-team briefings can be short and can/should occur at uneven intervals.
- Ensure all team members know they can call a briefing outside of upcoming scheduled ones (e.g., ones scheduled after a certain step in the SOP).
- Ensure members are talking with each other; they are not only speaking to the team leader or when called upon by the team leader.
- Recognize patterned behavior (e.g., the same team member always initiates briefings, or one member regularly provides information and another regularly seeks it). Such patterns both can indicate and result in poor team communication.

CHAPTER 10

HOW FLIGHT CREWS BALANCE PLANNING AND ACTING

LONG WITH BALANCING ROUTINES AND improvisation (Chapter 9), another tension to be addressed in teams facing critical events centers on planning versus acting. We have all spent uncomfortable time on teams that seem stuck in a planning quagmire, unable to move forward while the clock ticks away precious project time. The popular term "analysis paralysis" has been applied to many project teams. It might seem unintuitive, then, to think that teams not working under a set deadline—for example, a team facing a crisis situation—could be caught up in doing too much planning. It might seem that teams facing crises would naturally be compelled to act. In fact, would there not be a bias to do too *little* planning in a crisis situation? And *when*, during a critical event, would a team even find time to plan? These are the types of questions we asked with our colleagues when we began the study described in this chapter. How do low- and high-performing teams differ in terms of how they time their planning and acting during a crisis situation?

STUDY #2: COMMERCIAL FLIGHT CREWS[1]

The Setting. To examine these questions, we joined in a study, led by Dr. Zhike Lei, of commercial flight crews. As in the research described in Chapter 6, these flight crews also were engaged in interactive flight simulations. The design of these particular simulations, though, made this an ideal situation for studying our research questions. Specifically, each simulation contained a series of routine parts of a flight (e.g., standard preparation for approach and landing) along with nonroutine occurrences (e.g., crises—such as landing during manual depressurization). This mix of routine and nonroutine phases of the simulation allowed us to examine how these crews managed the timing and amount of their planning, despite being constantly engaged in task activity. With respect to this constant task activity, it is important to note here that these teams were constantly executing tasks during both routine and nonroutine parts of the simulation, and they did not have any breaks between these phases. Thus, these teams needed to figure out when to switch to planning while still performing tasks and remaining vigilant.

Our general prediction was that these experienced pilots would use the routine periods to assess the current situation and make plans about potential future scenarios. This notion is based on considerable evidence that the task and psychological demands of the nonroutine events can restrict attentional focus and decision-making capacity. In contrast, these resources should be more available during routine aspects of flights. Important to note is that we are not suggesting teams always act this way. Inexperienced teams may fail to plan during routine times and be left to do so during the most difficult and intense aspects of the crisis. Because the current crews were experienced, we regarded their performance as prescriptive—how teams *should* manage their planning versus acting.

Beyond wanting to know how and when these teams planned—versus solely acted—we were also interested in the question of *how much* planning teams should do. This study design was well-suited for studying this too. Because the study contained both types of phases, we were able to record how much time teams spent planning during the routine phase. We then correlated the amount of time different teams spent planning with their performance when needing to adapt to the subsequent nonroutine phase. Here, planning included team actions such as providing information and updates, and developing contingency plans, for purposes of coordination and preparation for expected or unexpected events.

The literature offered somewhat contradictory predictions for the relationship between time spent planning and ability to adapt during a crisis. Certainly, many studies confirm the intuitive notion that planning is essential for teams, and probably especially for those who may face complex and/or time-pressured events. Teams need to gather information about potential scenarios, discuss various potential strategies to address those scenarios, and coordinate who will do what and when during the execution of those strategies.

This said, more planning is *not* always better. More planning costs the team time that it could instead use to implement strategies. Also, more planning can result in—or be a symptom of—the team developing *too rigid* a plan or response—again, that concept termed "threat rigidity." Such plans can result in team member attention narrowly focused on remembering and coordinating each step of the protocol, at the expense of compromised situational awareness. With "blinders on," members may not recognize that their procedure needs updating, either because they misdiagnosed the crisis or because the crisis has changed and is no longer responsive to their original formation. Collectively, the team operates in a cognitive cocoon of sorts, as the crisis unfolds in a parallel reality of its own.

Combining these two ideas—that planning is necessary, but that too much could impair team adaptability—we ultimately reasoned that teams need to find the right balance of planning (versus acting or executing). This led us to

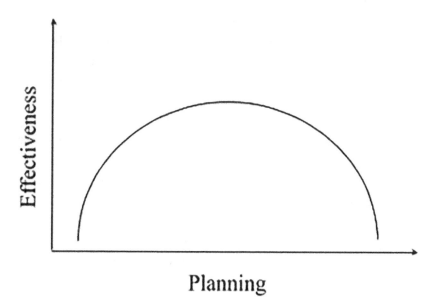

FIGURE 3.   Effectiveness vs. Planning.

think that there is a point of diminished returns in terms of how much planning teams should do when responding to a nonroutine event. Planning is
good, to a point. We depict this hypothetical relationship above.

Study Design. We studied eleven two-person professional flight crews
participating in a realistic, high-fidelity simulation. Each crew consisted of a
captain and a first officer. The participants were all licensed commercial pilots who flew for the same German airline. They were an experienced group,
with an average tenure of fourteen years in the aviation industry and an average age of forty.

The crews all flew in a full motion cockpit simulator of a Boeing 737–800
aircraft. The crews were aware that their simulator performance would have
implications for their professional credentials and/or organizational performance evaluations. Thus, although this was a simulation, it was a high-fidelity
one with important consequences for the crews.

As with the other studies in the book, our goal was to examine each team's
behaviors on a very micro level. Our microscope is one that focuses on the
series of hundreds of interactions and discrete team behaviors that occur over
the course of the event. In this case, the event—the simulation—lasted a little
more than an hour on average. During each simulation, the crew experienced
a series of routine and nonroutine events.

We audio-recorded each simulation, capturing each pilot's verbal utterances.
One key construct we needed to capture was the team's planning. Team in-
process planning refers to how teams analyze a changing situation and coordinate and strategize as events are unfolding. To capture this variable, we had
two trained coders listen to each simulation and record two critical planning
behaviors: *briefing* and *external communication*. Briefing entailed providing
updates, information, and anticipation for the purposes of preparing, and
coordinating for, planned or unlikely upcoming events. External communication occurred when one of the pilots interacted with other parties such as
flight attendants or air traffic control. Both of these behaviors entail collecting
information and sharing team plans to solicit approval or suggestions.

The other key variable we needed to capture was crew adaptation during
nonroutine events. To measure this, we had two aviation experts—an expert
airline training captain and a licensed pilot/Crew Resource Management
observer—rate adaptive crew performance. The experts made ratings for each

routine and nonroutine segment of the simulation. We averaged ratings across the two experts.

Results. The first question we were interested in was *when* did these experienced crews decide to engage in planning, despite always being engaged in task activity? To answer this, we first computed a ratio of the number of planning behaviors to the amount of time in that (routine or nonroutine) segment. Consistent with our expectation, these teams planned during the routine periods of the simulation more so than they did during the nonroutine periods. This result implies that the teams knew the workload and psychological barriers that the nonroutine segment presented (or would present) would hamper effective planning. They (wisely) planned when workload was lower, cognitive resources were likely higher, and attentional focus was probably broader.

The other question we wanted to answer was how teams balanced the amount of planning versus execution. We examined this by conducting a regression analysis, predicting expert-rated adaptive team performance with time spent in-process planning during nonroutine events. Interestingly, there was no relationship. This means that spending more or less time planning did not seem to translate into better crew adaptive performance. We then tested for a *curvilinear* effect (by adding a squared term to the equation). Indeed, this effect was significant, and the nature of it was consistent with our proposition. More in-process planning during the routine segments was better, to a point. After that inflection point, more planning was associated with *lower* adaptive crew performance. Whether implicitly or consciously, the more effective teams seemed to recognize that planning beyond a certain point would reduce the amount of time they had to implement their actions and/or lead to too rigid a response.

As we mentioned at the outset of this chapter, finding the balance is probably the most difficult of the three key ideas discussed in the book. Adaptability and appropriate timing are critical aspects of balance, but those are challenging concepts to master. Teams may be more easily taught to use closed-loop communication (Chapter 11), but teaching teams when to switch between planning and acting or how to ensure that interaction patterns fit the demands of a crisis is likely more difficult.

This said, teams need to learn all of these concepts—specific behaviors and how to use those behaviors in adaptable and temporally beneficial ways.

In Part IV of this book, we will discuss additional factors that can help you and your team enhance proficiencies. Below we provide a checklist based on what we have discussed in this chapter for use during a crisis.

Practical Takeaways for Chapter 10

- Ensure members are <u>exchanging information during periods of low workload and demand</u>.

  o These exchanges can involve subsets of team members or can represent whole-team briefings.

  o During these exchanges, team members should share their understanding of the scenario, what may happen next, what tasks they currently are performing, and what tasks they will perform next (depending on various contingencies).

- Teams should <u>develop initial plans</u> to address the crisis but recognize that *attempting to plan all aspects of the response is counterproductive.*

  o The nature of the crisis will continue to manifest as the team implements actions to address it. Also, teams simply cannot foresee all contingencies and potential actions needed.

  o Instead of trying to "perfect" an initial plan, encourage continuous reassessment of "what may be happening" and planning as the crisis unfolds. Use periods of downtime for these purposes (see point above).

CHAPTER 11

HOW MINE RESCUE TEAMS
GO SLOW . . . TO GO FAST

THE FINAL TENSION THAT WE IDENTIFIED AS critical for teams facing crises to balance is speed and precision. It may always seem a struggle for teams to fight against rushing through their work, given the overuse of team meetings and resulting distaste most of us now have for them. But particularly for teams facing crisis situations, the seemingly obvious need for immediate action may both overwhelm the desire to plan and also create one shared looming value: Time is of the essence. This value may make the faster-is-better assumption an unspoken yet incredibly powerful driver of team behavior during a crisis. However, and as we explored in the study we describe here, there may be evidence of a more *optimal* balance between speed and precision for teams facing critical situations.

STUDY #3: MINE RESCUE TEAMS[1]

The Setting. The final tension we describe is between speed and precision (i.e., accuracy and quality). To explore how successful teams managed this tension, we (Mary and Seth, with the help of our graduate students) studied Canadian underground mine rescue teams participating in prestigious annual provincial competitions. (We've presented this research at a peer-reviewed conference, and as of this writing, it is under review at an academic journal.)

Mine rescue teams are volunteer crews of miners and mining professionals who receive arduous physical and mental training to be able to respond rapidly and precisely to crises involving trapped or injured miners. Because of their extensive preparation and expertise, these teams are uniquely prepared and qualified to respond to mine emergencies. In most cases, they are the units called to rescue trapped miners (versus other highly trained response teams, such as firefighting crews or search-and-rescue teams).

Mine rescue teams date back to at least the early 1900s. Although mining has become much safer over the intervening years, these teams remain necessary given that mining is still a dangerous occupation, killing thousands of miners worldwide each year. Countries such as Canada, the United States, Australia, China, Poland, and others have many specialized mine rescue teams located geographically throughout their respective country that train regularly to respond to emergencies and rescue trapped miners.

Beyond their normal training, these teams often participate in mine rescue competitions. Many regions and countries hold internal competitions, and there also are international competitions, where the best mine rescue teams from around the world compete against one another. To be clear, the word "competition" definitely should not be interpreted as denoting "play" or "recreation" here. On the contrary, these competitions are physically and cognitively daunting. Simulations generally last between one and three hours. During them, team members wear full gear (including full-face oxygen masks) and carry very heavy equipment while responding to a series of extremely challenging events. These events might include putting out a fire to get access to an injured miner, or freeing a miner trapped under a fallen structure and then carrying the miner on a stretcher over a long underground distance of difficult terrain. The simulations contain elements such as fake smoke and actors (miners) who wear fake blood and are pinned beneath, or impaled by, (simulated) real equipment. To ensure fairness, the simulations are carefully scripted and choreographed, and their contents are kept secret until all teams have participated.

For our research, we were fortunate to observe a series of competitions coordinated by Ontario Mine Rescue (OMR) in Canada. In addition to observing the competitions, we had the opportunity to visit a nickel mine in Sudbury, Canada. Because this was such a unique opportunity, we need to mention a bit about our observations of touring a mine. First, we were shocked by the amount of activity going on underground. We did not expect to see huge trucks and machines passing each other on wide roads existing kilometers below the surface. Equally striking, though, was the utter darkness when we traveled to areas without any light from machines. As our guide told us, there is no comparable darkness; he was correct.

Study Design. We wanted to understand how successful mine rescue teams manage the tension between speed and precision. Specifically, we sought to determine how the most successful mine rescue teams communicated to achieve this balance. What kind of communication were they willing to sacrifice to gain precious time, and what kind did they deem too important to sacrifice—or even as ultimately buying them time (as *not* engaging in those communications would later cause team errors or worsen the crisis)?

We investigated this question by observing mine rescue teams competing in three province-wide annual competitions coordinated by OMR. Thus, this study took place over three years. These provincial competitions feature the teams that won their respective district mine rescue competitions (there are seven districts). Hence, of these expert teams, we were able to observe the most expert among them each year.

In total, we were able to observe and collect data from fourteen teams over these three annual provincial competitions. Collectively, the teams included ninety-eight miners organized into the fourteen mine rescue teams. These miners were experienced in mine rescue and in serving on their current team, as the average miner had been part of their team for almost seven years.

During each competition, the teams participated in a highly demanding and realistic scenario (different simulation scenarios were developed for each year). During the simulation, the mine rescue crew needed to respond to at least two major critical incidents. The simulation durations we studied averaged almost three hours. Each team consisted of a captain and a vice captain plus four other miners. In addition, each team included a briefing officer who remained on the surface to assist the team via radio communication with information from maps and mine schematics.

This team configuration resembles that of other teams we have described in the book. The captain here most definitely is nexus of the team. The captain coordinates and monitors the actions of the other underground miners as they work on their tasks (e.g., using various equipment to free and tend to a trapped miner) while also communicating with the briefing officer aboveground. Thus, the captain occupies a similar role as the primary/bedside physician in a trauma context and the unit supervisor in a nuclear power plant control room. During the simulations, the miners wore fire retardant suits and full-face masks, and carried breathing apparatus and heavy equipment, including a stretcher or "basket."[2] The simulations were conducted in darkened conditions with high levels of heat, to mimic real mine conditions.

The simulations were written by members of OMR to approximate real or possible scenarios, and were created to be deliberately complex and demanding. The teams were unaware of the nature of the narrative (i.e., situations they would encounter) until they began the simulation and the situation unfolded. Multiple experts from OMR were stationed along the simulation route in the mine and observed each team as it progressed; these experts judged each team on various performance criteria. After all teams completed the simulation (it typically took two days for all competing teams to go through the simulation), the winning team was announced.

In order to determine what kinds of communication teams used, we needed to record and then code team communication. The mine rescue team simulations were different from most others we had studied because they did not take place in a single, normal-sized room. Instead, the team moved around throughout the simulation, stopping only when they encountered an obstacle (e.g., a door they needed to remove) or an emergency to which they must respond (e.g., a trapped miner they needed to free). Thus, using a fixed microphone or following along with a video camera were not feasible options. Instead, we affixed a USB-drive-sized digital audio recorder to the inside brim of each captain's helmet. By later plugging this device into a computer, we were able to hear the captain's utterances as well as those of miners talking to the captain, including the briefing officer via radio.

Using transcripts of these communications, we were able to code the different types of communication utterances expressed by each team during the simulations. As with other studies, we coded for key types of team communication that are common during emergency scenarios and are important for team effectiveness. In total, we coded ten different types of communication. Because our interest was in examining the relationships between the frequencies of different types of communication and response time, we had to account for the fact that there was a "built-in" relationship between these factors; teams that took longer would communicate more—because they had a longer period of time over which to communicate. To remove this confounding variable, we computed the *ratio* of each type of communication by dividing the frequency of that type of utterance by the total number of team communications. We used these ratios instead of the raw frequencies in these analyses.

With these different types of communication coded, we could examine which were used more or less frequently by the especially fast teams. We just needed a measure of response time. We computed this as the number of minutes between when the team encountered the emergency event and when they had resolved that event. We were able to use the judges' time recordings of these two respective points to calculate the interval between them.

A distribution of the response times for the different teams suggested that there were two clusters of teams—one cluster who responded especially fast to the events and another cluster who did not respond as fast. We coded the two clusters of teams as 0 and 1, respectively. Using these codes, we then were able to look at mean differences in the frequencies of the ten coded communication behaviors. These analyses would tell us which types of communications the faster teams used more or less frequently than the relatively slower teams.

Results. Before getting to the results of these analyses, we should note two important points. First, the judges rated all of the fast teams as having performed adequately. This fact is important because it means that these teams did not just act quickly by making errors in a slapdash manner; rather, they acted quickly while avoiding excessive errors or problems. A second point worth noting is that, across various contexts, we generally do not find that the *amount* of communication is what matters for team crisis effectiveness—a result noted previously. *More* communication is not necessarily *better*. Armed with this knowledge, we were not expecting many differences in the frequencies of the various communication types between the fast versus slower teams here. In fact, we would not have been surprised if no differences emerged.

Our main analyses here consisted of a series of t-tests, comparing the two means of the two clusters on each of the ten coded communication types. The results are rather intriguing. Consistent with the point above and what we have found across different types of crisis-ready teams operating in dissimilar contexts, the amount of communication generally did not distinguish the teams who excelled during a crisis from other teams. In fact, of the ten communication behaviors we coded, there was only a statistically significant difference for two of them. These results are important as they provide further evidence, in yet another context, that more communication is not generally better. Faster teams did not share significantly more information, check in more, "talk to the room" (shout out a piece of information to everyone) more, or engage in more shared mental model development than the slower terms (in addition to other non-significant differences). The statistically savvy reader rightly may note that these t-tests were based on a very small number of teams within each group, resulting in low statistical power. This is a very valid point. Worth noting, though, is that the means for the fast and slower groups were almost identical for many of these types of communications. Paired with our similar past findings, these results suggest that any true differences are small indeed.

Equally interesting to us as these non-differences, though, were the two differences that *did* emerge. Results showed that the faster acting teams engaged in *more* of two types of communication than their slower counterparts. First, the faster teams used more closed-loop communication. In our coding protocol, we had defined closed-loop communication as "notice of understanding or reaction to receipt of information." Put simply, closed-loop communication occurs when the recipient of a message acknowledges receiving that message (or, further, demonstrates their understanding of what the message is intended to mean/convey). An example of closed-loop communication from our coding scheme was: "10–4." "Right on." In contexts like nuclear power plant control room crews, closed-loop communication is standard. There, team members use an extended form of it in which the original message sender "closes" the loop by acknowledging the recipient's acknowledgment of their original message.

The other type of communication that the faster teams used more frequently was explicit coordination. Explicit coordination includes gathering information and providing detailed guidance, especially outside of a standardized protocol or checklist. Explicit coordination represents the converse of implicit coordination, which we have discussed previously.

Initially, one might find these results strange or counterintuitive. These are communications that require time. They are detail oriented, and, arguably, might seem superfluous. After all, if Person A tells Person B to do something, and Person B is busy working on their own task, what is the danger of Person B's failure to acknowledge that they heard and understood Person A's request? As this example likely makes clear, the danger is that Person B did not, in fact, hear or understand the request. Seen in this way, the simple act of acknowledging the message (i.e., using closed-loop communication) is a manifestation of the team ensuring precision. And, that precision potentially could avert a major error or further deterioration of the situation. You likely do not need to be convinced of this fact. We all regularly have situations in which we believe someone heard or registered the information we provided (e.g., "Would you mind emptying the dishwasher for me?"), and the other person then reports never having heard us say it.

A similar logic holds for explicit coordination. As a critical care doctor once told us, sometimes you have to be direct when you need a team member to perform a given task during a crisis. While implicit coordination certainly can be beneficial in time-pressured scenarios, its utility relies on the assumption that the whole team is "on the same page" (i.e., has a shared mental model). Often, though, this is just not the case. If the team leader needs something done, telling their teammate explicitly to complete that task takes time, but it increases the likelihood that the task will be done. In contrast, if the leader had not said anything and the task was not done, the team may need much longer to later quell the crisis which, by that time, may have gotten considerably worse.

In sum, what our findings seemed to reveal was that fast teams managed the speed-precision tension in a very particular way. Although one initially might think of this as a "communicating versus speed" *tradeoff*, these results suggest it is not a tradeoff at all. The fast teams did not "go fast" in order to finish quickly. Rather, they "went slowly" by communicating in a deliberate and explicit way, in order to finish fast overall.

Important to emphasize is that these teams *did not communicate more.* They communicated more *in a certain way.* During the peak of a crisis, more communication may be harmful, not beneficial. As we saw in the German flight crew study, for example, most strategizing and planning should occur during relative lulls in the crisis, ideally not at the height of action periods. In this study as well, the faster teams did not share more information during their responses or engage in more planning than the slower teams. Rather, they expressed a particular type of information—direct and to the point—meant to promote coordination and avoid downstream problems during the response.

FINDING THE BALANCE SUMMARY

This chapter has shown the importance of crisis teams achieving balance. Over the last three chapters, we discussed three studies, each representing a different kind of balance that these teams may need to attain. We present the important takeaways, summarize results from the research investigations, and provide a section checklist in the following tables.

TABLE 9.   Finding the Balance Summary

	Type of Balance	Key Behaviors/ Indicators of Balance	Final Team Outcome
Nuclear Power Plant Control Room Crews	Routine vs. Improvisation	Adaptability—i.e., less patterned behavior; shorter, simpler interactions between team members; "communicate—act—communicate—act"	-Higher anticipation ratio (providing more information; requesting less of it) -Higher performance (as rated by training instructors)
Flight Crews	Planning vs. Acting	Planned for nonroutine events during routine phases of performance; Spent a significant amount of time planning before beginning to act	Expert-rated by instructors as effective (standard to outstanding) in preflight, takeoff, cruise, approach, and landing phases of flight.
Mine Rescue Crews	Speed vs. Precision	Use of closed-loop communication; greater explicit coordination (i.e., information gathering and more specific commands/guidance)	Time to successfully complete the two- to three-hour mine rescue simulation.

TABLE 10. Finding the Balance Checklist

Y or N	Behavioral Marker	Interpretation
	Team members "communicate— act— communicate— act. . ."	**Y** = Members are sharing information as (or before) needed, typically not with the whole team. This is in contrast to the team only communicating during whole-team briefings, occurring at set intervals. *If N . . .* • *Announce that communication can be ad hoc. Encourage members to provide information to specific other members before (or as) needed.* • *State that information must be shared immediately; team members should NOT wait for a briefing/meeting to disclose information.* • *State that more communication to the whole team is NOT necessarily better. Inform members to deliver information to those who need it, and only those who need it.* • *During briefings, discuss which team members will work with/ rely on each other for subsequent tasks (and thus information sharing). Be explicit about what information must be shared with the broader team.*
	Planning/ strategizing for potential crisis is done during routine performance events/phases.	**Y** = Team members are using opportunities marked by lower workload (and lower cognitive demand, time pressure, and frustration) so that they will be more prepared for crises, when workload, demands, etc. will be greater. *If N . . .* • *Initiate a briefing to plan/strategize for potential crises. Try to achieve the following during that briefing . . .* • *If time permits, consider having each team consider possible crises that may be on the immediate horizon AND each member's unique role in addressing those crises. Then, share as a team.* • *Discuss roles/tasks for potential crises. Have each team member describe their role and tasks AND what information they will provide others . . . and when.* • *Announce that the team will be using closed-loop communication from here on out (if the team is not already doing so).*
	Team members use closed-loop communication and explicit commands and information requests.	**Y** = Team members appreciate that using direct communication ensures information is heard and interpreted correctly by the intended other team member(s). *If N . . .* • *Announce that the team will begin using closed-loop communication (after training for its use).* • *Use team members' names when directing information to them or requesting information from them. Request acknowledgment of information. Monitor other team members to ensure this type of communication is occurring throughout the team.* • *If in-person, speak directly to team members. This is not the time to use a timid voice.*

Practical Takeaways for Chapter 11

- Emphasize (or even mandate) <u>closed-loop communication</u> during a crisis.

  o Recipients repeating each incoming piece of information they receive can prevent mis-communications that otherwise can contribute to the situation further deteriorating.

  o The use of closed-loop communication should be a standard part of crisis training. This said, there really is no reason it cannot/should not be used for "everyday" tasks too!

- <u>Be explicit and direct!</u> When you need a team member to carry out a task, directly ask the person to do so.

  o There should be an understanding among the team that members will directly communicate what needs to be done.

  o Create awareness that these communications should not be taken to imply that members are incompetent or need to be told what to do. If a team member fails to report task-relevant information (e.g., the task on which they are working), another team member should request that information.

- <u>Reject the notion that "more communication is always better."</u>

  o Team leaders (and trainers) should refrain from providing vague messages to "communicate." In time-pressured crisis scenarios, more communication is not necessarily better and can even be detrimental.

  o Instead, emphasize the need for closed-loop communication and explicit coordination.

PART IV

HELPING TEAMS BECOME CRISIS-READY

How Can We Best Prepare Teams to Face a Crisis-Filled Future?

CHAPTER 12

DESIGNING HIGH-PERFORMING TEAMS FOR CRISES

So far in this book, we have shared research evidence explaining the behaviors of effective teams during crises. Most of our examples have compared high-performing teams to low-performing teams in order to understand differences in team behaviors during crises. But how do high-performing teams become high-performing in the first place? Is it mostly luck? Do they happen to be composed of all extremely calm, capable crisis experts? Do their organizations somehow train high-performing teams differently than other teams? Do high-performing teams respond differently to training? Perhaps there are other major organizational factors that lead to these performance differences.

The prior chapters focused on exploring *what teams do to be effective during crises*. We have focused on the *behaviors* and *processes* that separate the teams that are successful from those that are not. But we have not discussed *why* the successful teams do those things differently in the first place. In the next three chapters, we explore some of the factors that explain why only some teams are more likely to consistently engage in the key adaptive behaviors during crises that we have described so far.

We start by discussing how *characteristics of individual team members*, such as skills and personality traits, enable the behaviors we identified in the previous chapters. We then describe how *team training* can facilitate these behaviors, and we explain how to develop the types of simulations that we have studied and created ourselves. Then we move on to discuss factors that lead to team resilience during the crisis.

TEAM COMPOSITION FOR CRISES: CHOOSING AND LEVERAGING MEMBER CHARACTERISTICS

Broadly speaking, there are two ways to develop or improve a team ahead of a crisis. One way is to identify and potentially select members on the basis of particular characteristics that will enable them to perform well during a crisis. These are characteristics that will help the team more effectively engage in the behaviors and processes described in the previous chapters. The other way is to train potential team members in those behaviors and processes. These two methods are what science supports.

Start with considering the individual characteristics that may enable team members—and thus the team—to engage in the key behaviors and processes we have already identified. Consider a quick thought exercise to make this practical. Take a moment and imagine that your team is facing a sudden crisis. Perhaps your organization's website suddenly goes down in the middle of a critical negotiation . . . or your team accidentally sends "you're hired" emails to the thousand applicants it meant to turn down. If something like this happened, to whom would you turn? Who do you count on to address crises?

A coach whose team is losing in the final minutes of a game will put on the field those players who have the capability to execute the needed behaviors. The coach knows who is fastest, who has the greatest leg strength, and so on, and will choose accordingly. Team members also have their own capabilities that will impact how they perform during crises. This all may sound obvious; it should. At the same time, few organizations or teams give much consideration to the individual attributes of members responding to crises until a crisis strikes, and sometimes not even then.

In a large company with many resources, the first step in response to crises such as those above might be to enlist help or even assign the crisis to others. In some organizations, for example, the role of "crisis management" is reserved for outside PR consultants. "I'd contact an IT expert if the website went down" or "I'd contact legal if my team sent the wrong emails to job applicants" may be the initial response of some. However, these responses assume that such resources outside the boundary of the team are competent, available, and willing to help, particularly if the responsibility for addressing the crisis lies squarely with a team. Also, each second of delay during a crisis could cost the organization money and reputation (and a few jobs). Even if a leader is not in the position to make those calls and has little say in who is working along-side them during a crisis, we suggest there is *much* value in knowing what key characteristics of oneself (and one's potential teammates) are linked to enacting the key behaviors identified in the previous chapters.

What are these important individual characteristics? The field of industrial-organizational (IO) psychology provides a systematic approach to thinking about this question. First, determine what key behaviors individuals will need to accomplish successfully. Then, work backward to identify the attributes that allow individuals to achieve those behaviors. This all may sound intuitive, but organizations often get it wrong. They often compose teams based only on individual performance. In order to compose a team capable of facing a crisis, they choose high-performing individuals—those people who are, in particular, very good "technical task" performers. Technical tasks involve knowledge and information connected to taskwork, while teamwork tasks involve coordinating and communicating with other team members.

Making team composition decisions based *only* on individual technical task performance is very similar to the fallacy of the "Dream Team." The

---

Technical Tasks

- Involve using specific trained information or knowledge to directly address the crisis
- Examples: Getting the website back online, tactfully contacting the applicants who were misinformed, resuscitating a patient
- Requires specific expertise

Teamwork Tasks

- Involve communicating and coordinating with other team members
- Examples: Balanced communication, setting the tone, helping behavior, information sharing, using closed-loop communication, updating shared mental models
- Enactment of these behaviors/processes facilitates effective taskwork by ensuring that the right people do the right thing at the right time

---

FIGURE 4.   Technical and Teamwork Tasks.

popular press is full of sports examples of teams filled with great individual performers who could not coordinate and work together. A team of super-stars, though impressive in other ways, is often very far from what a crisis situation demands.

In the preceding chapters, we described many research studies of teams staffed by trained professionals with very high levels of technical task exper-tise. These individuals were certainly selected as team members at least in part due to this expertise. It is obviously important that team members' levels of expertise meet the threshold necessary for them to perform the tasks associ-ated with both routine and nonroutine situations. However, managers and organizations often place too much emphasis on technical task expertise and not enough on the ability of team members to engage in the teamwork tasks vital for team effectiveness under stressful, uncertain conditions. For example, aviation safety improved dramatically after the late 1970s and early 1980s with the advent of Crew Resource Management training that encouraged open, trusting communication between captains and first officers—who were high in technical task expertise—thereby reducing human error and improving teamwork task performance in flight crews.

Teamwork Tasks. In the past chapters, we have described team processes that underlie team crisis response, and the behaviors that constitute those pro-cesses. These behaviors and the processes they create are among the precise ones that constitute the nature of teamwork. Achieving effective coordination, communicating appropriately, engaging in collaborative problem-solving, knowing when to strategize versus act—behaviors such as these are the es-sence of teamwork.

TEAMWORK KNOWLEDGE AND SKILLS

How do we know which individual characteristics enable individuals to communicate more effectively, know when to strategize versus act, and so forth? One place to start is by considering generic teamwork competencies. Researchers have developed surveys to measure people's teamwork knowledge and specific teamwork skills. For instance, to measure teamwork knowledge, people can be asked standardized questions with correct answers. Here is a sample question:[1]

Suppose that you find yourself in an argument with several co-workers about who should do a very disagreeable but routine task. Which of the following would likely be the most effective way to resolve this situation?

   A. Have your supervisor decide, because this would avoid any personal bias.

   *B. Arrange for a rotating schedule so everyone shares the chore.

   C. Let the workers who show up earliest choose on a first-come, first-served basis.

   D. Randomly assign a person to do the task and don't change it.

FIGURE 5.   Sample Question.

You could take surveys like this yourself to assess your own teamwork knowledge and skills, or do this along with your teammates if you are part of a permanent team. The goal here is to identify who would benefit most from training on which particular knowledge and skills.

Generic teamwork knowledge and skills should help you and your team execute some of the processes and behaviors outlined as critical in past chapters. However, they are not meant to be crisis-specific. In our research, we have identified some individual attributes that may map more directly onto these fundamental aspects of crises.

TIME URGENCY

One of the central aspects that we have alluded to in several studies concerns the timing of key crisis behaviors. In multiple studies, results showed that teams need to move rapidly in executing certain behaviors. For instance, in Chapter 6, we reported that high-performing crews tended to prioritize tasks or distribute tasks immediately after the verbalization of a nonroutine event. Why do certain teams move more rapidly than others? One likely reason is something called *time urgency*: These teams have members who are more time urgent. Time urgency is a personality-like characteristic. People who are time urgent (or time aware) focus on time; they check the time frequently and know exactly how much time they have until deadlines. Individuals who are less time urgent are not as focused on the passage of time; deadlines seem to "creep up" on them. If you would like to measure your or your team members' time urgency, we have included a reference to one time urgency survey in the endnotes.[2]

Being time urgent is not always a good thing. In fact, time urgency is re-lated to a sense of chronic hurry and, not surprisingly, to stress. But during a crisis, the presence of urgent people on a team has some real benefits. These individuals tend to view time as "the enemy"; in a crisis, it typically is. Because time urgent team members are more attuned to the passage of time, they tend to act quickly. These are the folks who will distribute and prioritize tasks right away. In contrast, less time urgent individuals can lure the team into think-ing it has more time to complete the tasks than it really does. We're sure you all know "crammers" who either forget about deadlines or mistakenly judge that they will have enough time to get everything done when starting later.[3] Crammers present problems for all kinds of teams, but probably especially for teams facing crisis situations, when the team will not have time to catch up.

Because acting quickly is important, having some people who will pro-pel the team toward fast action is generally helpful. We say "generally" here because we also have pointed out that faster is not always better for all crisis behaviors. In Chapter 4, we discussed that higher-performing seaport crisis management teams spent more time in the information sharing phase, ensuring that they were considering and disseminating all of the necessary information. Similarly, in Chapter 10, we presented data showing that the flight crews that adapted best to nonroutine events spent a moderate amount of time strategiz-ing beforehand; they did not cut off discussion prematurely.

Collectively, these findings suggest that while having time urgent indi-viduals is helpful to push the team toward action, the team also needs to maintain a focus on the broader temporal landscape. The solution here is not to try to balance the perspective of time urgent team members with less time urgent ones. Instead, we suggest considering two other personality-like traits that we have identified in our research as important for maintaining a more global focus on time.

TIME PERSPECTIVE

The first of these two characteristics is called *time perspective*. Time per-spective is a natural human attentional bias that we all have; it concerns what temporal area we tend to focus more on: past, present, or future. Research-ers have discovered that individuals differ in how much we focus on the past versus the present versus the future.[4] For instance, you might know some people with a more past time focus, always recalling days gone by, when their children were young and at home, or maybe about their glory days. You also likely know people "living in the future," perhaps with lofty expectations about days ahead or, alternatively, fixated on potential perils years to come. If you would like to assess your own time perspective, check out the article by Philip Zimbardo and John Boyd.[5]

Unlike time urgency, there is not one type or level of time perspective that you should necessarily seek for your crisis team. Rather, some research has suggested that teams containing members with divergent time perspectives perform best in crises.[6] This is because such diversity would allow the team to achieve greater situational awareness. Members deep in task engagement would benefit from being present-oriented. This orientation will provide situational awareness of the immediate task situation. These individuals will help your team as it engages in current tasks, but they tend not to think about what will happen in the future. Meanwhile, members with a more past focused time orientation could gain insight from similar past scenarios. Finally, those with a future time orientation anticipate and strategize about what may lie ahead. So, while time urgent individuals are pushing the team to "move faster, move faster," members with a future time orientation will consider how the team should strategize to combat what might arise later during the crisis. Notably, these actually could be the same people who are time urgent; these are separate characteristics.

POLYCHRONICITY

The other time-related characteristic we have identified as being beneficial during a crisis is called *polychronicity*. The term may sound technical, but the concept is not. Polychronicity refers to the preference to multitask—that is, to continuously switch among multiple tasks. Some people prefer working this way. If you are someone who checks email, works a little on a task, goes back to checking email, makes a phone call, then goes back to your task all in the span of a few minutes, you likely are polychronic. Alternatively, if you prefer to complete a task fully before moving on to your next task, you are more monochronic. Obviously, sometimes we need to do things a certain way for reasons beyond our control (e.g., think getting ready for work in the morning while preparing children for school). But people still differ in their preferences. We include a reference to an article with polychronicity survey items.[7]

The academic literature suggests that whether being monochronic versus polychronic leads to better performance depends on the nature of the task. For crises, though, being more polychronic would seem beneficial. This is because many crisis situations involve continuously switching among tasks and between periods of strategizing and intense action (as we discussed in the study of flight crews in Chapter 10). In these situations, team members need the cognitive flexibility to switch from task to task as the situation demands. Also, as we have suggested elsewhere, polychronicity can function both at an individual level and as a team-level phenomenon.[8] Thus, having members who prefer to multitask not only increases the likelihood that these individual switch among their own tasks, but it also shifts the team's collective work to be more polychronic. Finally, we also should note here that time urgent people seem to facilitate *less* polychronic team behavior.[9] Instead, time urgent individuals tend to shift the team toward being more monochronic, insisting the team finishes one collective task before moving on to the next one. This strategy may be useful for some team tasks, such as when the team needs to concentrate together and keep on task. But that seems less of a concern in many crisis situations. Rather, the team often needs to multitask, with subgroups of the team working on multiple tasks simultaneously; polychronic individuals are the ones who will initiate those shifts.

In sum, as we discussed in previous chapters, team crisis behaviors related to timing are critical, and these three attributes—time urgency, time perspective, and polychronicity—relate to appropriate execution of these time-related behaviors.

POSITIVE AFFECTIVITY

There is one other individual attribute we have discovered through our research that impacts team effectiveness during crises. It is called *positive affectivity*, often referred to as just PA. Before describing what PA is, we first describe why it matters during crises. As we have mentioned at various points in the book, crises are emotional events. They often evoke stress, but they can also elicit other emotions such as anxiety, frustration, despair, and sometimes even hope and team pride. These various emotional responses have important implications for many of the key behaviors and processes we have described so far. For instance, it is well established that stress narrows attention, making situational awareness and coordination more difficult. When an individual is very stressed about something, they may become intensely focused on that thing and attend less to other circumstances. Now imagine trying to lead a team in which everyone is stressed with their attention narrowed, yet you need them to gather and share information quickly in order to update the team's shared mental model and keep everyone moving in the same direction. It can be challenging.

Positive affectivity is a personality-like characteristic that relates to how people view the world and which types of emotional experiences they tend to have. Individuals higher on PA view themselves and the world favorably, and they tend to be more enthusiastic, excited, and generally happy. Those lower on PA are more sluggish and apathetic. They just don't get very enthused by much. Think Tigger versus Eeyore here.

On might anticipate that *more positive* is better. That is not what we found in our research. We also did not find that *less positive* is better. In a study of nuclear power plant control room crews working during realistic simulation crisis situations, we found that the best performing teams were those with members who had *similar* levels of PA.[10] It did not matter if the members were universally positive, universally bored and sluggish, or somewhere in the middle; what mattered was the *similarity* of the members' PA. Why would this be? Likely, it is because this characteristic represents—or informs—part of that lens through which each of us interprets and reacts to events. When team members have very different lenses about emotional events such as crises, it can create friction. Indeed, we found here that part of the reason more emotionally diverse teams performed worse was because the members were especially frustrated during the simulation. For team members who tend not to show emotion, it can be frustrating to work with people who do, and vice versa. In turn, it seems likely that such frustration could make shared situational awareness, coordination, and similar team-work behaviors a challenge.

TEAM MEMBER FAMILIARITY

Before we conclude this chapter, we must emphasize an additional quality that is important for team composition: how familiar members are with each other (i.e., how frequently they have worked together, especially in responding to crises). Unlike the other qualities we have described, familiarity obviously is not an attribute of a single individual. Rather, it is the property of a team (or some subset of the team, such as when particular members are especially familiar with each other).

We emphasize familiarity because many studies show the benefits of team members being familiar with each other for important outcomes. On a project led by Dr. Sarah Parker on team familiarity and surgical outcomes, we used electronic records of thousands of procedures to show that surgical teams in which members had operated together more frequently (i.e., greater team familiarity) tended to complete procedures more quickly.[11]

The benefits of team members having worked together more frequently likely accrue because team members have already learned who knows what and who can do what (i.e., the team has a transactional memory system), and they are familiar with each other's idiosyncratic behaviors. Members better can predict how one another will react and behave during the crisis and thus can adjust their own behavior accordingly. One does not need to be part of a team facing a crisis to notice this phenomenon. For example, you likely have a good sense of how your close friends or family members tend to behave during get-togethers, and you very well may adjust your own behavior accordingly. The simple takeaway from this research is to try to create standing crisis teams, where members train together and are ready to address real crises together. Obviously, though, things are not always this simple. In many contexts, having the same set of people ready to respond to crises is not feasible. An example of this would be commercial aviation crews, where pilots typically fly with pilots and crews they have not flown with before. In other cases, familiarity is not possible because the organization needs to bring in outside members (e.g., experts) to deal with particular crises. We discuss ways to train to compensate for a lack of familiarity in Chapter 13.

At the end of this chapter, we present a table summarizing the personal characteristics we have found beneficial for teams addressing crises. We would add two points about this table. First, this summary is based on our focused findings about teams facing crisis situations. One should bear in mind that there is a voluminous, much larger research literature on team staffing and composition. Also, we recognize that staffing teams to meet *all* of the criteria listed here would be difficult to achieve in practice. Teams facing crises may be staffed based on technical expertise, job position, or, as often happens, chance. Still, we suggest that inspecting this list of attributes (and the measures of them) can provide insights that otherwise may not have occurred to those charged with creating such teams. Also, doing so can facilitate thinking about how to compose teams in conjunction with training them to deal with crisis situations effectively—the topic of our next chapter.

TABLE II.   Effective Crisis Teamwork

All team members should have **Teamwork Knowledge and Skills** (e.g., in communication, coordination, planning).

Consider having at least some team members who are more **Time Urgent.**

Consider having a team diverse with respect to members' **Time Perspective.**

Consider having team members who are more **Polychronic** than Monochronic.

Consider having team members with similar levels of **Positive Affectivity.**

Consider having team members **Familiar** with each other (i.e., optimally, have worked together and/or handled crises together, either in actual or simulated situations).

CHAPTER 13

TRAINING HIGH-PERFORMING TEAMS FOR CRISES

IN ADDITION TO CONSIDERING TEAM COMPOSITION, perhaps the most fundamental way to prepare teams to face crisis situations is through *team crisis training*. In general, teamwork training is growing business; for example, according to a 2022 report on workplace trends based on use of its online learning platform, Udemy Business reported a 129 percent increase in interest in the topics of teamwork and communication.[1]

In the corporate world, teamwork training often takes the form of organizational development specialists or management consultants conducting half- or full-day workshops. These workshops obviously vary in many ways, but they almost invariably include attendees completing a series of "team-building" activities. One common activity involves groups of colleagues discussing which items they would bring with them if they were sent on a mission to the moon together, or, less cheerfully, if they were marooned on a desert island. Another popular activity is to have groups try to build the highest or longest structures, using materials such as marshmallows, dried pasta, or paper clips. After the groups complete these latter exercises, the facilitator often announces that groups of children build better structures than adults, because children experiment more and care less about ego than do adults. In other cases, training consists of colleagues participating in "ropes" courses or adventure courses to hone their teamwork skills (think "trust fall" here).

Such activities can build camaraderie, forge new relationships, and sometimes provide useful insights about teamwork. However, there are more targeted alternatives to these exercises if the specific goal is to help a team function well in a crisis. If you want to prepare a team to effectively handle a crisis, there is a straightforward training approach to follow: train, and provide feedback on, the behavioral competencies the team will need during a *crisis*, and have them practice these competencies in a setting that simulates key crisis conditions. If a crisis is likely to involve angry stakeholders, simulate the situation by including dealing with realistically angry tweets, emails, and phone calls. If a crisis is likely to involve making decisions under time pressure, include time limits in your simulation tasks. Firefighters train by running up flights of stairs carrying equipment and by carrying out weighted "victims," often in structures simulating burning conditions. Nuclear power plant control room crews train by responding to simulated crises in exact replicas of the control rooms they operate in every day; these mock control rooms include loud alarms, ringing telephones, flashing warnings—the sensory inputs a crew would face during an actual crisis event. All of these example teams train by engaging in the behaviors they would use during an actual crisis, in a context very similar to the one in which they would use them. We suggest that teams likely to face crisis situations train following a similar approach.

Several years ago, one of us was asked to talk with a professional racing pit crew that was having difficulty performing during races. The crew seemed to perform fine during its training, but would fall apart during actual races, with crew members bumping into each other, dropping equipment, and costing precious seconds that the manager felt led to lost races. The crew trained wearing most of their normal gear in a semi-realistic mock-up of a real racing pit with a race car that would scream into the pit; crew members jumped over the wall just like they would during a real race, performed their tasks expertly, and the car screamed off, usually without a problem. Then we started asking questions. What was different between race day and training? What did the crew members smell, hear, see, and taste that was different during a race that they didn't experience while they were training? It didn't take long to get the answers. During training, there was no screaming crowd, and particularly, no screaming fans just feet away yelling obscenities at the crew. There was no manager yelling in crew members' ears through the built-in communication system in their helmets. And there was no fog of smoke from the track to confuse everything. After our conversations with the crew, speakers were set up in the practice pit to pipe in crowd noise, and fake smoke was blown in during the training sessions. We are unsure if the crew started playing recordings of the manager's voice in their helmets during training or not. With time, the crew's race performance improved dramatically.

These team training prescriptions—making acute situations in training as similar as possible to real conditions—may sound obvious. At the same time, few organizations follow them. Only a very small minority of organizations follow these principles and, among this minority, the training is usually reserved for their top management teams and teams responsible for maintaining critical processes.

This scenario is problematic. In its annual report on organizational training, *Training* magazine—a top trade journal about workplace training—regularly reports "increasing the effectiveness of training programs" as the top priority among the organizations surveyed.[2] If those same organizations are using activities in which groups of kindergarten children outperform working adults who should be experts at their jobs, this finding is not surprising. Training takes time, and costs money (over ninety billion dollars annually, across organizations, in fact).[3] If twenty-five organizational members participate in a two-hour teamwork training session, that is fifty hours of collective work time lost and fifty hours of pay. Our suggestion is simply that teams and organizations might as well use that time and money on training that will translate to clear benefits when it really counts—like during a crisis. And if more training is needed to adequately prepare an organization for a crisis situation, it is not only a solid investment, it is also—as we underscore more completely in Chapter 15—an *ethical* investment.

If our assertion above makes sense and team training for crises seems like a logical approach, how does one make this happen? While offering a complete how-to guide for creating and implementing a simulation-based team crisis training program is beyond the scope of this book, in the following pages, we briefly describe the basic elements of such training. As evidenced in the research studies we have previously discussed, simulations are an integral part of training for virtually all teams charged with handling potential crises in high reliability contexts and extreme environments. This is not surprising, as research shows that simulations yield greater learning and skill acquisition than do traditional education and training strategies.[4] Between the two of us, we have had the opportunity to observe hundreds of training simulations across a range of contexts. We have also created team-based simulations for crisis management classes, and we have written with co-authors on how to design crisis management simulations for education.[5] We attempt to impart an overview of what we have learned from these experiences below.

STEP 1: DECIDING WHAT TYPE OF CRISIS TEAM EXISTS AND WHO TO TRAIN

One initial decision to make is who will participate in a simulation. We suggest that there are two major considerations guiding this decision. First, and most importantly, who participates in the simulation training largely depends on which individuals would respond to the potential crises you may encounter. In fact, one purpose of the simulation is to help determine who that might be. Considering various types of potential crises (see below) often reveals connections an organization should make or strengthen (e.g., with a particular department or other organization) in preparation for a particular type of crisis.

The second consideration in determining who to train, and also in determining what that training may look like, concerns the type, or configuration, of the crisis team. At this point, it may be helpful to refer back to our discussion of different team configurations in Chapter 1. The focal distinction we wish to emphasize here regarding those different types of crisis teams pertains to team familiarity. As we outlined in Chapter 1, some teams are fairly stable; a designated crisis team such as a top management team who regularly handles the organization's "big fires" would be an example of a team where membership is stable. In contrast, for other teams, membership varies. Members may have worked together only once or twice or perhaps never at all until responding together as part of the team combating the current crisis.

Why is thinking about these different types of teams important when considering who participates in crisis simulation training? First, doing so reveals that training is an excellent opportunity to *develop* familiarity in the types of teams where members would otherwise remain unfamiliar to each other until the real crisis occurs (e.g., ad hoc crisis teams). That is, organizations can use simulation training to introduce individuals who do not regularly work together but who plausibly may be called to work as part of the same team if a (particular type of) crisis did occur. As we described in Chapter 12, team members being familiar with each other's work styles and other attributes generally yields better team outcomes. Simulation training should be a place where individuals from different shifts, departments, and disparate areas of an organization—who reasonably may be called to work together during a crisis—should train as a team.

A second, and corollary, implication of considering the different types of crisis teams here is that there are some cases in which simulation training cannot be used to develop familiarity. For logistical (or other) reasons, developing such familiarity simply is not feasible. This is indeed the case with commercial aviation. Commercial pilots fly with too many other pilots to train every possible combination. Ideally, the simulation training would include all of these individuals; clearly, this is not possible. Aviation's solution has been to train everyone (e.g., all pilots) in the same highly standardized teamwork principles and practices (Crew Resource Management, or CRM) and to reinforce their use. This could be called the "plug-and-play" approach; if a set of behavioral competencies (like Setting the Tone, Adapting on the Fly, and Finding the Balance) is well trained across a wide group of potential team members so that these behaviors serve as a common language during a crisis, this shared behavioral understanding makes up for any lack of familiarity on the team. This approach can be tremendously effective, and it can substitute for the value of members already having worked together multiple times. But we also want to emphasize that simply training this approach is not sufficient. An organization or industry needs to have a very strong culture that essentially mandates behavioral competencies. Aviation and some other industries have embraced that type of culture. Some other similar disciplines have implemented CRM-like training but have not quite succeeded in achieving this cultural aspect, at least not yet.

STEP 2: DECIDING WHAT TO TRAIN

We now turn to designing simulations. To help make this discussion more clear, we will reference a simulation that Mary, along with colleagues Dr. Zhike

Lei and Robert Pratten, described in a publication, based on a simulation that Mary designed to use in her MBA crisis management classes.[6] Mary has gone on to design several additional simulations for executive MBA courses using this technique. As in most any learning/training process, the first step is defining the learning objectives: What is it that you want participants to get out of this simulation training? These objectives need to be specific and measurable. An objective of "improving teamwork" generally is not sufficient, especially absent corresponding metrics to track changes in teamwork. An appropriate question to ask at this point might be, "Which of the various behaviors discussed in the preceding chapters should be prioritized with this training?" After all, we have described many behaviors and team processes; attempting to design a simulation that offers stimuli or opportunities to engage in too many targeted behaviors could simply be too much for team members, leading to feelings of being overwhelmed or resulting in members shutting down or self-censoring. Instead, by focusing on a few targeted behaviors and building a scenario around them, the training experience can be made realistic and memorable, and the learning points clear.

Beyond training specific and discrete behaviors, however, is the notion of training teams in the competency of adaptability—key in facing crisis situations. As we have stated previously, trying to precisely predict and train for specific crises can be nearly impossible; thus, we want teams to possess the capabilities and competencies needed in order to face and adapt to *any* crisis that comes their way. By training teams with recurrent simulation training that exposes them to different scenarios and problems, we help teams and team members build expertise in both the behavioral competencies and adaptability that set high-performing teams apart. As teams become practiced in dealing with sudden changes, in shifting their mental models as the situation evolves, and in quickly reprioritizing tasks, they also become more desensitized to encountering crisis events. Desensitization refers to a psychological process of becoming less distressed as a result of repeated exposure, and it can help teams retain their focus during actual crises.

In our crisis management class simulation, we had several learning objectives. We wanted the student crisis management teams to experience a situation in which developing and updating their situation understanding and mental models was critical, and in which the sharing of information through a transactive memory system was also critical. Thus, we developed a simulation that allowed for the demonstration and evaluation of these specific behavioral competencies. For instance, the real-time, fast-paced nature of the simulation necessitated the use of precise information sharing and implicit coordination. We also stopped the simulation at a few points and queried team members with a quick online quiz to assess their knowledge of team crisis management principles (or "declarative knowledge") previously presented in the classroom that were directly applicable to the simulated situation at hand. The most important lesson here is that there needs to be alignment among the learning objectives, the content of the simulation, and the assessment. The behaviors that are the focus of the simulation should be based on learning objectives, and the simulation should include opportunities for teams to engage in those behaviors so that they may be assessed.

STEP 3: WRITING THE SIMULATION NARRATIVE

There are various ways to decide on the type of crisis narrative you will model. In industries such as aviation and nuclear power, simulation trainers often write simulation narratives based on real crises that have occurred somewhere in the industry. Sometimes one can borrow from a crisis to re-create the story in a different industry; for example, Mary has created one crisis simulation narrative loosely based on the Volkswagen "Dieselgate" scandal (i.e., falsifying diesel emissions tests), instead using the setting of a large defense department contractor that falsified data from its proprietary virtual reality headset designed to train military personnel in target acquisition skills.

One common practice is for trainers to begin with one potential (or experienced) crisis and then add to it one or more other elements to increase the overall complexity or challenge of the simulation. For example, a simulation narrative might begin with the crisis involving a leaked internal memo that puts an organization in a very bad light. Add to this the posting of the memo on social media and the involvement of an antagonistic activist investor. The idea here is not to model every possible permutation of the crisis; that is obviously impossible. Rather, the goal here is to "stretch" team members and increase their adaptability.

Our crisis management class simulation narrative involved a bomb threat in an underground mine. We considered three possible narrative structures for the simulation: sequential, branching, and dynamic (see the following figures). The sequential structure shows three sample decision points (type of mine closure to enact, type of bomb squad to use, and whether to release a press statement). Each has multiple options, but all options with a decision will lead to

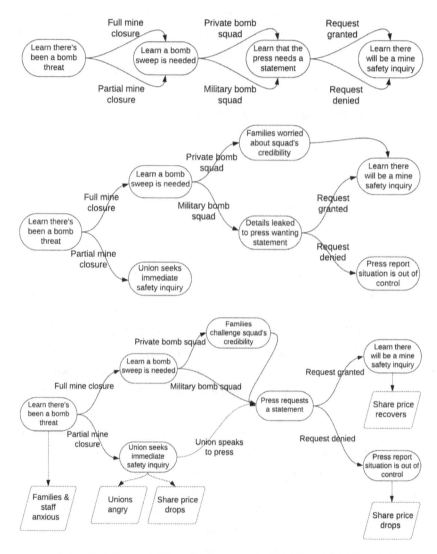

FIGURES 6–8.   (top) Sequential Narrative Structure. (middle) Branching Narrative Structure. (bottom) Dynamic Narrative Structure. Permission courtesy of the Academy of Management Learning & Education.

the same endpoint. The branching structure has the same decision points but includes a different outcome for each decision option a team might choose. Finally, dynamic structure is the most interactive. It includes more behavioral choices and also includes differing information given to participants at points, during the simulation, depending on their chosen paths.

Our team ultimately chose to use the sequential structure that combined the sequential eight-decision-point storyline with dynamic external information received by the crisis teams at certain times. So, even though the outcomes were the same regardless of the decisions each team made, the simulation included multiple opportunities for information collection and the proactive exchange of information with different stakeholders. Having the opportunity to demonstrate these behaviors mapped onto the learning objectives of the simulation.

STEP 4: CHOOSING THE CONTENT AND DELIVERY OF THE SIMULATION

Guided by the narrative, use content (e.g., emails, phone calls, texts, "actors" bringing messages to the team) and the timing of this content to make the simulation a dynamic experience. Think broadly about what your crisis will entail, what content and what internal and external stakeholders will be involved, and how you can incorporate the content and stakeholders into your simulation. You will have to think differently here, as the "taskwork," which is usually of priority, may play backseat to the teamwork that underlies it. Thus, for instance, we might use time until a patient is intubated as a measure of team effectiveness in a trauma simulation. But the time to complete this task largely depends upon the coordination of the team. So, the simulation should require coordination throughout in order to reach that technical endpoint.

For our crisis management class simulation, the team members were assigned the role of vice presidents in a top management team for Blink Mining, a fictitious organization that owned a mine where the bomb threat was occurring (i.e., the crisis). We created a website for this organization, showing the firm's operational strategy, financial information, and historical information (in the form of fake press releases). Each member was assigned a role on the team about a week before the simulation began (e.g., VP of Operations,

VP of Finance, etc.) and were given some unique information pertinent to their departments in the organization. Thirty minutes before the simulation began, participants were told that the Blink Mining CEO would be flying to Europe, and thus unavailable, for the next several hours.

The entire simulation lasted about two hours. During this time, participants received various electronic pieces of information at predetermined times (delivered to their personal university email accounts, texted to their phones, and via their social media accounts). Each message was sent automatically, not by humans (see the article for software details), ostensibly by a stakeholder.[7] For example, an "irate investor" sent emails to the Vice President of Finance when the stock price of the firm sank. In response to each message or event, the team needed to make several decisions under severe time pressure. For instance, they needed to decide the type of evacuation plan to implement, the type of bomb squad to use for a sweep of the mine, whether to grant a media interview in response to a reporter's request, whether and how to respond to angry employee social media posts, and so on. These decisions were made in a context that necessitated team situation awareness and flexible interaction. Failure to respond to an inquiry in a timely manner would result in automatic negative feedback from that stakeholder. Also, the teams received a television "breaking news" broadcast story about the bomb threat that increased the time pressure and need for a public response. When the simulation concluded, the crisis teams received an email from the CEO asking them to develop and send her an action plan for Blink to implement within the next twenty-four hours, and giving them thirty minutes to do so.

We provide a detailed account of this simulation training narrative to give you a sense of what type of experience is possible to create without investing millions of dollars in building a mock control room or full-motion flight simulator. There is a truly endless number of possibilities of what simulations like this one could resemble; the content, media, and "actors" involved in simulations can be represented via messages delivered through emails, via texts, or by actors on live video. The point is that the upper limits of realism and "high fidelity" may not be necessary in order to create the environment and opportunity for teams to engage in the behaviors you wish to target; nor is ultimate realism necessary in order to create, and thus desensitize, the stress of facing an unexpected crisis event with a team.

A good example of a low-fidelity simulation that many team trainers use—including Seth and colleagues—is a "tabletop" exercise.[8] In a tabletop simulation, participants (e.g., members of different public agencies) discuss how they would coordinate and respond to a particular crisis such as a natural disaster or mass shooting. Going back to what we said above, the learning objectives need to drive the simulation. Tabletop exercises can be extremely useful for purposes such as creating interagency protocols and chains of command, and for revealing holes in current ones. They generally are less useful, though, than the more dynamic, higher-fidelity simulations (like the one described above) in terms of enhancing team adaptation and focusing on the execution of specific behaviors under stress and time pressure.

STEP 5: EVALUATING LEARNING FROM SIMULATIONS

In order to assess the learning that has occurred, the behavioral outcomes from the simulation should be measured, based on the original learning objectives. As with creating the simulation, there are many options here. Unfortunately, evaluation of simulation training efforts is often given too little attention, or none at all. Having participants respond to surveys about how helpful they found the training is better than nothing, but this is still far from satisfactory. The research on evaluation is very clear that these reports are not accurate assessments of learning. We discuss some additional methods here.

One option is in-the-moment feedback. In fact, one real advantage of behavioral simulations is that they allow for real-time assessment and feedback. What we mean by real-time assessment is simply the notion that simulations can be suspended briefly for evaluation and immediate learning. For example, in the nuclear power plant control room simulations we have observed, stopping simulations briefly is common practice; this way, the expert trainers can intervene and ask questions about an operator's or the crew's actions. This is best practice and is consistent with research evidence supporting the use of immediate feedback for learning and improved performance. The manner in which these mini-learning sessions are executed also matters. The trainer should refrain from first imparting their wisdom. Rather, they should query the team members, seeking to understand their situational awareness and the reasons for their actions. Such questioning will usually reveal where gaps in awareness or behavioral understanding exist; these holes then become the learn-ing targets. One specific example of this practice we have observed entails the trainer privately asking each team member to report their current situational awareness—that is, their understanding of what is occurring in the crisis situ-ation, and what the important team goals and tasks are at the moment. Very often, this exercise reveals that team members possess very different under-standings of the situation, and this creates a learning opportunity regarding building and updating shared mental models.

In addition to these in situ learning sessions, trainers may ask simulation participants and/or expert team observers to complete surveys afterward about the team's proficiency on the targeted processes and behaviors. Researchers have developed several excellent surveys that assess many of these variables.[9] However, surveys do not capture the actual verbal and nonverbal behaviors that ultimately constitute what team members, and teams collectively, do dur-ing crises. As made clear in the description of our studies, we believe knowing what actual behaviors occur—what team members do—is key to understanding team performance. To illustrate the value of behavioral observation, contrast team members' opinions of how adaptable their team was during a simulation versus seeing a timeline detailing each discrete behavior team members engaged in over the course of a simulation. The former is recollection and opinion; the latter captures the variability of the team's different actions across the dura-tion of the crisis, which *is* adaptability. Thus, we strongly recommend video-recording simulations and using the video to code (i.e., note the incidence and time) the verbal and nonverbal behaviors you focused on training in order to construct such a timeline. Much more information on behavioral observation methods like these is available in our article on the topic.[10] Video excerpts can also be used in debriefings, which we discuss next.

STEP 6: DEBRIEFING/AFTER-ACTION REVIEWS FOR LEARNING

After the simulation concludes, there is an essential final step: completing a debrief. Debriefs, somewhat similar to after-action reviews (AARs) or "ho-twashes," are a critical part of team training. Of all the various components that could impact the effectiveness of simulations—the logic of the narrative, the cognitive and sensory realism or fidelity of it, and so on—research consistently shows that whether or not there is quality debrief is the most critical component for learning and future performance.[11] Of importance, we have chosen to mention debriefs in the context of simulations, but debriefs should also follow the conclusion of any real crises that a team experiences.

Other researchers have defined a debrief as "a systematic technique that turns a recent event into a learning opportunity through a combination of task feedback, reflection, and discussion."[12] The U.S. Army developed AARs in the 1970s as a way to facilitate learning from combat exercises. In the intervening decades, debriefs and AARs have become common in other industries facing nonroutine events too. They now are standard practice in aviation and nuclear power, and have become increasingly common in healthcare organizations.

The army emphasizes that the purpose of the AAR is to determine (1) what happened, (2) why it happened, and (3) how to improve or sustain collective performance in the future. We note here that the "what" and "why" are perhaps especially important, yet difficult, to answer for crises. This is because of the complexity and ambiguity inherent in crisis events (Chapter 1). While debriefs and AARs for some training may reveal straightforward answers to these questions, discussions about what happened during a crisis and why things unfolded a certain way require depth and expertise. If everyone on the team immediately agrees about the nature and causes of the crisis and the team response to it, this very well may signal the need for further digging.

Debriefs and AARs are both past-oriented, covering and making sense of what occurred, and future-oriented, capturing what needs to be trained or done differently going forward.[13] In addition to facilitating feedback, debriefs should include two other components. One of these is observational learning. Observational learning entails reviewing the simulation (e.g., the video recording of it, performance metrics) and modeling correct or appropriate actions that were, or should have been, taken. Second, a goal-setting component should reflect the degree to which simulation performance met the levels set for the learning objectives and also set new objectives (and associated metrics) for future training.

Importantly, having the team members themselves conduct a debrief seems to be more beneficial than having experts (e.g., supervisors) do so. This likely is because having "external" stakeholders present can make members more hesitant to speak up and acknowledge errors they might have made. It also can make simulation participants reluctant to ask questions that could show their lack of knowledge. Put simply, having outside members lead the debrief limits team members' sense of psychological safety.

Returning to the bomb threat simulation that Mary and colleagues conducted with MBA student crisis teams, debriefs were conducted with the teams in class, following the simulation. During the debrief, the teams were shown measures of their performance (e.g., average time until they responded to stakeholder queries, the number of unsolicited messages teams sent to stakeholders, graded scores for the content of teams' messages) as well as the narrative and timeline of the simulation events. Following this, the teams met for twenty minutes to reflect on their performance and pinpoint both the most significant challenge the team faced as well as the best decision they made. After each team shared their reflections, there was a class-wide discussion about linking certain simulation outcomes to the simulation learning objectives. For instance, students noted connections between the average time taken to make critical decisions and to respond to external inquiries with transactive memory systems and team situation awareness.

We want to emphasize that debriefs are essential to team training and learning; they amplify the value of simulation training manyfold. For further information on the topic, the extensive work of Jenny Rudolph and colleagues on debriefing provides a good starting foundation.[14]

Before concluding the chapter, we should note that training is the most proximal route to develop the behavioral competencies teams need during crises. While composing teams that already possess certain characteristics (as described in Chapter 12) will also provide team benefits, some of those characteristics (e.g., diversity in members' time perspective) seemingly are less directly related to team effectiveness than are the specific team behaviors and awareness which can be trained.

In Table 13, we provide a summary of the steps involved in designing and conducting simulation-based team crisis training as described above along with important considerations and recommendations at each step. We also provide a checklist for those engaged in designing and evaluating simulation training. In the following chapter, we discuss one of the positive outcomes of solid team composition and training practices: team resilience.

TABLE 12.   Team Crisis Training Checklist

Contextual Factors/ Strategies	Specific Actions to Take
Team Crisis Simulation Design Team Crisis Simulation Debriefing	• *First define specific learning objectives. Also determine how you will measure those objectives and what the desired level of proficiency is/looks like.* • *Determine what kind of team you likely would be working on during a crisis (e.g., dual-purpose stable team, etc.; see above). If you are likely to be part of a team in which people do not know each other, the importance of discussing specific expertise and roles becomes even more salient.* • *Design the crisis event so that it is aligned with the learning objectives. Multiple opportunities to demonstrate each behavior/process should be built into the simulation.* • *Define performance metrics associated with various behaviors/processes— that are aligned with the learning objectives.* • *Write a script using past or imagined crises, or reimagine a crisis from a different context.* • *Conduct a thorough debriefing session in which team members reflect on the simulation and their actions and then set goals for future improvement. Ensure participants feel safe to discuss mistakes, errors, and gaps in knowledge.*

TABLE 13.   Simulation Steps for Team Crisis Training

Steps	Considerations and Recommendations
1. Deciding What Type of Crisis Team Exists and Who to Train	• Determining various types of crises your team/organization may encounter and who would staff those teams. • Considering the types of teams you will train. Can you use simulation training to facilitate familiarity among potential crisis teammates? If crisis team membership will be ad hoc/variable, train for standardized ways of communicating.
2. Deciding What to Train	• Establishing learning objectives. Considering whether the focus is on training specific behaviors, general teamwork principles and concepts, and/or desensitization/habituation to stress. • Ensuring there is alignment among the learning objectives, the content of the simulation behavior/performance.
3. Writing the Simulation Narrative	• Considering crises that others in the industry or in the region have experienced. • Layering crises by incorporating unusual pairings of events in order to increase team adaptability.
4. Choosing the Content and Delivery of the Simulation	• Considering various types of formats and technologies (e.g., press conferences, texts, emails, social media posts) to which the team needs to respond. • Ensuring that the simulation is sophisticated enough, but not more sophisticated than it needs to be.
5. Evaluating Learning from Simulations	• Considering multiple methods to evaluate individual and/or team execution of the targeted behaviors. • Considering coding team behavior (if resources allow) to use for research, training, and development purposes.
6. Debriefing/After-Action Reviews for Learning	• Ensuring a "no-blame" climate during debriefs/AARs, and ensuring all members feel psychologically safe to explore errors and to offer suggestions and feedback.

CHAPTER 14

ENHANCING TEAM
RESILIENCE FOR CRISES

A FINAL FACTOR IN TEAM EFFECTIVENESS during crises is team resilience. These days, talk of the importance of resilience seems to be everywhere. One cannot avoid the word. It is the focus of self-help books and podcasts; leaders discuss it in emails and meetings; and virtually every academic discipline now seems to feature articles on resilience in some way.

One important implication of this exponential proliferation is that the term is used in many different ways to connote various ideas or concepts. For instance, resilience sometimes refers to a team (e.g., that *is* a resilient team), sometimes to the property of the team (e.g., that team *has* resilience), sometimes to a process (e.g., that team has *built* resilience over time), and yet other times to the successful outcome of experiencing adversity (e.g., that team *was* resilient). Related to these distinctions, resilience sometimes refers to a latent *capacity* to handle potential adversity that has not actually occurred, and other times it refers to actually *being* resilient during adversity that has occurred. In this latter case, success in dealing with adversity may lead to inferences about the latent capacity the team always seemingly possessed.[1]

The term arguably has become so differentiated in both common parlance and academic literature to become borderline meaningless. As an illustration of this notion, imagine a team leader encouraging their team to be resilient during a crisis. How are team members to interpret this message? Is the leader encouraging members to forge ahead during the crisis, weathering obstacles, without seeking help from each other? Or perhaps the leader is suggesting the team should adhere to the decided upon strategy, despite members' misgivings about it? Alternatively, maybe the leader is merely trying to inspire the team to succeed, using resilience as a rallying call of sorts. Team members could have any of these interpretations or others. Of course, members' interpretations do not necessarily converge with each other's or with the leader's intended meaning . . . assuming the leader even had a clear one in mind.

Given this accumulation of meanings and resultant state of affairs, we want to be clear about what we mean by team resilience in this chapter. First, our focus is on *team-level* resilience, not individual-level resilience. Particular individuals in the team may be, or act, more or less resilient, but team-level resilience represents a property of the collective unit. As we discuss next, this emergence results from, or represents, the joint influence of various factors, including member characteristics, the training they have received in preparation for the crisis, and the resources the team possesses to address the crisis over time.

What exactly do we mean by team resilience? Let us start by describing what we do *not* mean. Resilience is not invulnerability to crisis. To be resilient is not to be immune to crises. To the contrary, as we will discuss, resilience entails being crisis-ready. Being resilient also is not defined as having successfully weathered crises. We do not view resilience as an outcome or attribute that only can be assigned after a team has experienced and addressed a crisis. Rather than these treatments, our conceptualization of resilience prioritizes vulnerability and recognizes that the latent readiness to experience crises precedes success in handling them.

We regard resilience as a *dynamic capability* of teams—one that, if managed appropriately, can be tapped and continuously renewed over time: before, during, and after particular crises. This portrayal emphasizes adaptability, treating resilience both as a latent property of the team and also as an emergent and dynamic one that is responsive to both external and internal factors (e.g., changing environmental demands and team capabilities). Being resilient means being vitally prepared for adversity. This conceptualization is very similar to the definition of resilience that Kathleen Sutcliffe and Timothy Vogus provided after they had reviewed various definitions of the concept, as "the maintenance of positive adjustment under challenging conditions" (p. 95).[2]

Many writers have compared being resilient to the properties of a rubber band. Using this metaphor, we can imagine a team being stretched to fit and cover the challenges it faces, and then relaxing, recovering, and renewing between challenges. But let's take this metaphor one step further, and imagine a rubber band that doesn't lose its elasticity and eventually crumble and break over time, but instead actually adds to its ability to stretch and recover each time it is used. That's the conceptualization and manifestation of dynamic capability we see in truly resilient teams.

Throughout this book, we've highlighted evidence-based behaviors that high-performing teams use to successfully meet a variety of crisis situations. We've organized these behaviors into three categories: Setting the Tone, Adapting on the Fly, and Finding the Balance. Now imagine the teams in our studies dealing with those types of unpredictable crisis situations again and again over time, just as many teams in real organizational settings must do. Why are some of these teams—even the high-performing ones—more *resilient* over time than others?

Below, we elaborate on three key elements of this formulation of team resilience.

ELEMENT 1: POSSIBILISTIC THINKING IN RESILIENCE

The term "resilience" often evokes the portrayal of one successfully navigating hardship. If we are asked to think of resilient people we know, the individuals who come to mind likely have overcome much adversity. This certainly is one part, or conceptualization, of resilience. But, if we think about "success" a bit more broadly, another fundamental part of resilience becomes apparent—that of avoiding adversity, or minimizing its potential impact, in the first place, before it (may) occur.

This recognition implies that resilience is not simply about what happens during or after a crisis; it is a continual state of readiness and adaptability. One implication of this view of resilience—as a sustained state reactive to dynamic changes—is that it can make crises, and thus team crisis response, less relevant. Put simply, much of resilience is about adjusting to seemingly small system perturbations and installing proactive mechanisms to prevent the emergence or escalation of full-scale crises—what is termed second-order problem-solving.[3] Taking this reasoning a bit further, the most salient examples of what we typically think of as resilience—defined as successfully weathering adversity—sometimes represent cases of lacking resilience using the conceptualization presented here.

Now, this all may make a lot of intuitive sense. An ounce of prevention is worth a pound of cure, as the saying goes. Applied to teams facing crises, such prevention would entail scanning the environment for possible crises and preparing for them. Indeed, this approach captures how organizations typically prepare for crises. They rely on past events, those that have befallen others in their industry, and perhaps "close calls" to forecast the likelihood of certain future crises. They then devote resources to mitigate the occurrence and severity of such crises. Sometimes this forecasting is done formally, aided by statistical modeling, and other times less formally, relying on what "comes to mind." This type of preparation represents what crisis management expert Ian Mitroff refers to as *probabilistic thinking*.[4] Such thinking entails trying to predict which particular crises the organization or team is most likely to encounter and to then prepare for (e.g., train, gather expertise) those specific crises.

Probabilistic thinking is essential. To be sure, teams have some foresight about which crises they are more likely to encounter. As such, devoting resources to those types of crises is clearly a worthwhile strategy. Teams who regularly encounter crises implement this kind of thinking and preparation systematically. Firefighting crews prepare for fighting various different types of fires, accounting for structure type, environmental conditions, and other fire characteristics. Similarly, analyst teams serving the intelligence community constantly scan for different impending threats and train for those potentialities.

But this prescription to "scan and plan" using probabilistic thinking only gets a team so far. The fundamental problem with relying only on such thinking is that it leaves much of the potential crisis space unseen. Teams plan for the crises they have observed (or learned of), forgetting that what has occurred represents only a fraction of what may occur. It is as if one is always looking at the lighted side of the moon, failing to realize, or believe, there is another (darkened) side. Unfortunately—and partly owing to it remaining unexamined—this darkened side often contains the most damaging crises.

Why do many crises go unseen until they occur? There are several factors that explain this phenomenon.

First, as we have emphasized throughout the book (see Chapters 1, 13), thinking we can predict exactly which crises a team will encounter—and thus need to prepare for—is a fool's errand. Many of the most damaging crises represent scenarios that we never could have foreseen. They were simply unthinkable. With the advantage of hindsight, we may see them as having been predictable. However, we cannot fathom all that may occur. We tend to forget that past crises were once unimaginable too. In the days following the deadly 2023 wildfires in Maui, Hawaii, for example, the governor was asked why the state was not more prepared, to which he responded, "We've never experienced a wildfire that affected a city like this before."[5] Similarly, nuclear plant managers had greatly underestimated the possibility of a tsunami causing a meltdown until the 2011 Fukushima nuclear disaster in Japan.[6] These situations reflect the reality that many of the most serious crises are ones we fail to see coming.

Also, crises often reflect the convergence of various elements in unknowable ways. Although we might have been able to foresee each of these components in isolation, we could not have predicted them coalescing in these ways. This notion bears some resemblance to what is often referred to as the Swiss cheese model of organizational safety/accidents.[7] This model emphasizes that disasters result from a series of "aligned" holes (think of pieces of Swiss cheese aligned such that one could place a pencil through aligned holes among them). The model has been used to explain various accidents such as the Chernobyl nuclear incident and the Exxon Valdez oil spill. While the model offers practical implications for "closing" those holes, it also highlights the challenges—if not the impossibility—of planning for every combination of causes that could lead to a crisis.

A related difficulty in forecasting crises is that no two crises are identical. Even among crises of the same type, each particular occurrence of that category has its distinct idiosyncrasies. Each car accident to which firefighters respond can be seen as a variant of the infinite number of car accidents that can occur. The same is true of ethical scandals and financial ones.

Indeed, this is one of the reasons that much of the research on crises takes the form of case studies; researchers generally go into great depth trying to understand a particular crisis to derive general concepts rather than trying to compare across different real-world crises. So, while a team certainly can (and in many cases should) train for particular types of crises, the ones they will actually face almost invariably will differ in important ways from their training.

Compounding these difficulties in predicting the nature of specific crises are the various biases we operate with when considering even those crises we reasonably could accurately foresee. Perhaps most problematic among these biases is our tendency to believe that each of us is immune to particular adverse occurrences, a phenomenon termed "unrealistic optimism." We all know that divorces, heart attacks, and serious illnesses happen, yet we systematically underestimate the probability that we will experience such events.[8] Of course, we may not experience any of these specific occurrences in our own lives. But as the list of possible adversities increases, so too does our chance of encountering any one (or more) of them. Eventually, everyone faces major challenges. But how do we know which ones to prepare for, especially when we tend to think none in particular will befall us? The optimistic bias also acts to color our perceived ability to deal with crises. Teams that have been successful may believe they always will be.

It should become clear fairly rapidly that accurately predicting all crisis events that might occur is impossible. Although we do have the responsibility to prepare for known events—events that have a likelihood of occurring, such as a salmonella outbreak at a food processing plant—we often cannot fathom the next crisis; it simply is outside the schema we possess for what may occur. We also tend to believe we are relatively impervious. We know that a sexual harassment scandal or building fire or major fraud case in the media *could* happen here, but we reason it never will. Our company is too successful or too big for a crisis to befall or seriously hurt us; our employees are dedicated and want the best for the company; we have standard operating procedures to handle all crises; we could control the media to avoid a crisis; we can recover from anything; and so on. We ignore, rationalize, assume the best . . . until we are proven wrong.[9]

Given these challenges, how then are organizations and teams to prepare for such crises? What is needed is a shift in how organizations, and their constituent crisis teams, think about and prepare for potential crises. Instead of only engaging in probabilistic thinking to prepare for crises that reasonably may occur, teams and organizations also need to embrace what Mitroff calls *possibilistic thinking.* In this type of thinking, one considers what possibly *"could"* happen by considering potentialities that have never manifested and by combining elements of past crises that possibly could co-occur in the future. We want to emphasize that the goal here is not to conceive of every possibility. Again, there are some possibilities that defy imagination and more combinations of foreseeable events than we could fathom. Considering every possible crisis is neither possible nor essential. Rather, this type of thinking has two key benefits.

First, engaging in possibilistic thinking unearths scenarios beyond those that occurred previously. The hypothetical crises one generates may not map directly onto one that ever actually does occur, but such imagined possibilities certainly will expand the space of potentialities beyond relying just on historical data. Such exercises "stretch" our thinking about what could happen. One great example of such an exercise is the metaphors exercise developed by Carol Cirka and Elizabeth Corrigall—an exercise that encourages thinking beyond cognitive biases and boundaries in order to imagine possible crises.[10] Furthermore, engaging in such thinking through structured exercises facilitates further similar thinking going forward; it encourages a growing awareness and consideration of how each element in one's work environment has latent potential to contribute to crises, partly by interacting with other elements.

Following from this last point, a second benefit of such thinking is that it helps organizations move from a crisis-prediction model to a *crisis-readiness* stance. Instead of only readying for particular crises, possibilistic thinking facilitates a mindset that crises always are around the corner and that the team (or organization) should prepare for various types of crises or, put differently, for crises in general. This type of thinking focuses on capabilities—*on developing an adaptive set of behaviors* that will pay off during *any* crisis—rather than trying to predict exactly which crises are going to occur and when, like a roulette wheel. Crises are no longer seen as possible once-in-a-lifetime occurrences that may manifest but hopefully will not. Rather, crisis preparedness is built into teams' everyday existence and functioning. Teams expect to handle crises and prepare continuously for them. It is through this regular awareness and preparedness that such teams both avert crises and are more ready when they do occur. In Table 14, we suggest five specific exercises to help develop possibilistic thinking.

TABLE 14.   Possibilistic Thinking

Use Pre-Mortems	A pre-mortem involves imagining crises (or failures, etc.) and thinking about why they occurred. It involves asking "Why did this (imagined) outcome happen?" and "How can we take preparative steps given this knowledge?" This is in contrast to an after-action review, which focuses on determining why actual crises, etc., occurred and on deriving and implementing lessons learned.
Use Daily Challenges and Workarounds to Unearth Potential Crises	Consider the daily challenges in the work environment and how those might contribute to crises. These can be seemingly mundane challenges (e.g., traffic leading to many employees being late to work, or employees not having someone's cell phone number). Consider how these challenges would contribute to, or worsen, a crisis. Also consider workarounds. These are strategies workers have developed to "get around" problems or challenges at work. They can be very effective but also can reveal underlying latent problems that could contribute to or amplify a crisis.
Use a Crisis "Grab-Bag" Exercise	Have participants list potential challenges or crises. These can include specific crises (e.g., the CEO is arrested) and seemingly more frequent problems (e.g., there is a power outage in the community and employees cannot access their Internet). "Grab" several of these items repeatedly to create different combinations of crises to consider.
Use Metaphors	Use the metaphors exercise described and cited in Chapter 13.
Use a "Wheel of Crises"	Create a wheel with different categories of crises to which teams may need to respond (e.g., normal, abnormal, and natural accidents). This looks like a spinnable disc. Have team members first think of examples of each category. Then, have members combine examples from the different categories. This method is explained expertly by Ian Mitroff and Can Alpaslan in the article cited here.[11]

ELEMENT 2: TEAM STAFFING FOR RESILIENCE

A second element of team resilience is having the appropriate personnel available for crises. We already have said much about this topic and provided practical recommendations in Chapter 12. Here, we supplement that discussion with an eye toward facilitating team resilience in particular.

As emphasized in Chapter 12, decisions about staffing teams likely to face crises depend partly on the particular type of team configuration/type (see Chapter 1). That said, some principles apply across teams. One is that teams should be composed of members with a mix of technical knowledge and skills. As we described above, predicting the specifics of crises to which teams will respond is not particularly fruitful. For this reason and for many crisis situations, team members collectively need to possess a diverse set of technical capabilities. For baseball fan readers, we think of a pitching bullpen as a useful analogy. A team wants a diverse reservoir of pitchers in the bullpen from whom they can choose to pitch, depending on the game situation. Similarly, a crisis team should have access to a reservoir of potential members with varied knowledge and skills from whom they can draw.

A second principle that applies across types of teams is that redundancy in staffing is beneficial. Having two surgeons on staff who could perform a specialized operation is better than having one, for obvious reasons. Having multiple people who can access a certain drive is useful because the one person who has access may be away. This is a simple notion. Yet we have seen examples where this straightforward principle is not applied, leading to problems for teams. In offering this recommendation, we recognize that it may seem contradictory to the first principle—that of striving for diversity in team member capabilities. However, short of every member being an expert on everything (which becomes increasingly impossible in highly specialized scenarios), our suggestion is to strive for both diversity and redundancy, finding a balance between the two criteria.

A third principle related to team staffing is that teams need to consider adjustments to their team composition during crises. Crises evolve; thus, the team that first arrived or was chosen to address a given crisis very well may not be the most appropriate team to handle it later. Adjusting team membership sometimes means adding experts with unique knowledge of the unfolding scenario. Sometimes it means adding, or joining, whole other teams that will be (or have been) addressing other parts of the crisis already. This resultant structure is called a multiteam system, where teams of teams need to coordinate, while each team also must internally coordinate.[12] At still other times, this adjustment can mean shedding team members. This is rare in our experience, but perhaps should not be so rare. We have witnessed healthcare situations where over ten providers rush into the room when a code (i.e., crisis) occurs, some mainly just to observe. Having a reservoir of capable team members to staff teams is preferable, but having more team members operating at a given time than is necessary is not preferable for many kinds of tasks.

In any of these cases, the coming and going of team members requires coordination and information sharing. Skills will be lost and gained, as will specific knowledge about the crisis scenario, as members transition on and off the team. Furthermore, new members typically benefit from adopting the same shared mental model that existing members possess. However, there often is not ample time to brief them as they enter the scenario. Instead, this act must occur rather seamlessly, with the necessary information being transmitted until a break allows for fuller briefing and information sharing. We have likened this to a band playing a concert, and then an additional performer being called onstage to join the band "mid-jam" without anyone skipping a beat.[13] Or, if you are a hockey fan, you might think of coordinating a "line change."

There are various strategies to help with these adjustments or transitions. First, as we described in Chapter 12, having members who already are acquainted with each other can minimize missed or misread cues important for the development of shared mental models. Second, member expertise is essential here. Team members with high levels of expertise can often quickly diagnose a situation and determine a course of action; they can see patterns and holes, even if they can't always articulate what they are seeing.[14] As such, transitioning into a new and dynamic team situation is much easier for them. Finally, training for these adjustments is very beneficial. Returning to the hockey metaphor, hockey teams of course practice line changes, and so should crisis teams. In many healthcare organizations, clinicians now do something similar to routinizing handoffs when patients transition between providers; by routinizing and standardizing these important transitions, the thought is that fewer errors will occur. During crises, though, the transitions often are chaotic, occurring under extreme time pressure and producing incomplete and/or contradictory information. As such, training to help team members become more familiar with their execution during larger crisis events is also important.

ELEMENT 3: CREATING CRISIS-READY CONTEXTS AND SYSTEMS

The third element of building and maintaining crisis team resilience is creating a team context that embraces the possibilities of crises. Central to this element is a shared mission of continuous learning and improvement among team (and organizational) members. Team and organizational leaders must emphasize that learning and improvement require knowledge of current problems as well as potential ones. Such problems include system issues, errors one has committed (or has seen others commit), and foreseeable dangers.

This element is both a result of, and is manifested in, the systems and incentives that organizational and/or team leaders put in place. For such systems to be effective, they must be nonpunitive. Mistakes, errors, and the like are seen as normal and inevitable. The same is true of inefficient work systems or procedures. They are not admissions of inferiority or weakness or criticisms of one's colleagues or supervisors. Rather, reports of such incidents or problems are seen as opportunities to learn, to improve, and to avoid larger crises. Some industries have embraced these notions. For example, many airlines have systems in place in which pilots report near-misses. Healthcare increasingly has adopted systems like this too, implementing anonymous procedures for staff to report problems and concerns.

Such learning takes place not only before crises but after them as well. This occurs in the form of after-action reviews and debriefs, as described in Chapter 13. The lessons learned from these sessions then represent an input into other systems, such as staffing and training. Of course, most learning that occurs will not be the results of a full-blown crisis. Thus, there need to be mechanisms to incorporate the feedback from the "small" problems detected into the team and organizational systems as well. Too often, this latter process does not occur. Instead, only major crises trigger changes. This can readily be seen after any major disaster. The organization, media, and lawmakers call for immediate changes to systems. Sometimes, of course, these changes are warranted. Oftentimes, though, such entities did not devote resources or attention to solving the small problems that could have averted such a crisis.

In closing this section, we also need to emphasize that there is an entire field of study devoted to business and organizational continuity that deals with systems and resource redundancy. Eliminating hazards that potentially could lead to crises and also building rigorous and redundant systems to prevent full-scale crises certainly are essential elements of crisis preparedness. Because excellent resources already exist, we do not elaborate on these factors here. See the endnotes for recommended resources for interested readers.[15, 16] In the following figures, we present a summary of the points discussed in this chapter and summarize the team crisis resilience process.

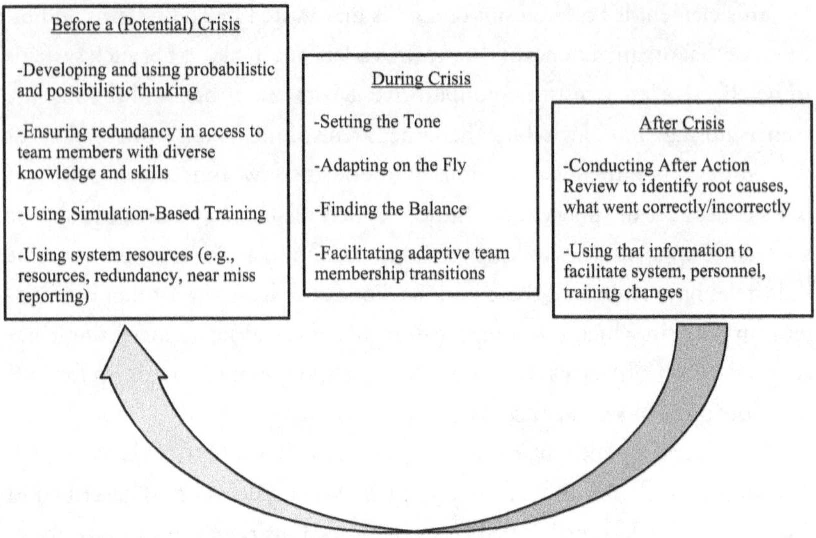

FIGURE 9.   The Resilience Building Process.

Practical Takeaways for Chapter 14

- To prepare for potential crises, rely on both probabilistic thinking and possibilistic thinking. For the latter, teams and organizations can use the exercises described earlier in this chapter. Depending on team type, members of a given team or members of various units/agencies (who potentially may form a team) can develop possible scenarios.

- These scenarios then can inform the development of simulation-based training. Regardless of the crisis scenario, though, training for resilience means emphasizing the principles of:

  o Setting the Tone

  o Adapting on the Fly

  o Finding the Balance

  o Facilitating Adaptive Team Membership Transitions

- Teams and organizations also can use the scenarios derived from these two types of thinking to consider gaps between current and potentially needed expertise when responding to crises. Strive for both diversity and redundancy in knowledge and skills in potential teams. Also use these exercises to identify potential sources of such capabilities beyond the immediate context (e.g., organization, locale).

- Build a crisis-ready context by emphasizing the inevitability of potential crises. Implement a system for organizational members to anonymously report errors, potential hazards, workarounds, and wrongdoing. Hold regular discussions where each member discusses errors they have made and describes conditions and scenarios they could foresee contributing to crises.

CHAPTER 15

THE ETHICS OF CRISIS PREPARATION

At the height of the COVID-19 pandemic, certain product seemed to fly off store shelves, creating immediate shortages as the public struggled to stay safe and wait for a vaccine. Toilet paper seemed to be in perpetual short supply along with another product that everyone seemed to chronically seek: hand sanitizer. Retailers' supplies of hand sanitizer could not be replenished by their logjammed supply chains, and what little of the product available for sale was sometimes going for gouged prices on the Internet, if it could be delivered at all.

Enter a surprising rescuer: craft distilleries. Many small distilleries found that with some small changes, they could pivot from producing their regular offerings of small batch whiskey, rye, vodka, and gin to bottling the hand sanitizer that their communities so desperately needed. And many—if not most—of these small businesses gave away their small batches of hand sanitizer rather than sell it, seeing the switch to sanitizer not as a way to survive the crisis economically, but instead as a way to help their suffering patrons, local police departments, hospitals, and surrounding communities at large. And this, even though the

*distilleries were experiencing significant losses due to their tasting
rooms and bars being closed during the pandemic.*

*When asked about his decision to give away his distillery's hand
sanitizer, one owner put it very simply: "'The community has
supported us, so it's an obligation, if you have a product that
could be helpful,' he said. 'It's what you do.'"[1]*

* * *

What powerful words: *"It's what you do."* To us, these words refer to the ability
of the distilleries to adapt and turn on a dime during a crisis, but also indicate
that the view their leaders saw from the top reached well past the boundaries
of their organizations and extended out to the communities that lay beyond.
Exceptional situations sometimes produce exceptional actions.

Throughout this book, we have focused on sharing information about
the behaviors that teams and their leaders can use to be more effective during a crisis situation. Teams are most organizations' "first responders" during crises, whether they are permanent teams with stable memberships or
ad hoc teams composed of the people who happen to be present when the
crisis hits. And as we have pointed out, those teams in crisis-prepared organizations are in a much better position to respond and adapt to whatever
the turbulent world presents them than are those teams embedded within
crisis-prone organizations.

We discussed the evidence-based methods we have used with our research
partners to identify the vital behaviors of effective teams, and how our approach differs from several others. We described specific behaviors that effective teams are likely to use near the beginning of crisis situations (Setting
the Tone), while a crisis is unfolding (Adapting on the Fly), and periodically
throughout a crisis (Finding the Balance). We also discussed how organizations can help increase the likelihood that their teams will be effective during
crises (Helping Teams Become Crisis-Ready), with a heavy emphasis on team
composition, training, and resilience.

But for an organization and the teams embedded in it to really be effective during a crisis, and for an organization to arrive at the state of being
crisis-prepared, it takes visible and consistent commitment from the top.

Crisis preparation is not something that can be completely turned over to a consultant or a single employee, and it is definitely not found in an old crisis plan (usually stuck in a dusty binder) that has not been updated or even looked at in years. Real crisis preparedness must become a baked-in element of the organizational culture. Increasingly, boards of directors are requiring management teams to make demonstrable commitments to crisis preparation, but people can still readily sniff out the difference between a CEO and top management team going through the motions versus really engaging and believing in crisis preparedness.

PREPAREDNESS SPILLOVER

Such true engagement benefits the organization more than many executives realize. We have already outlined in Chapter 13 how simulation training can help inoculate teams through desensitization when it comes to decreasing the experienced threat, fear, and stress of a crisis situation. And we mentioned in Chapter 1 how such training can build in the "muscle memory" capabilities of communication and coordination that teams need for any crisis they might face. Other aspects of anticipatory preparedness, as we have discussed, might involve top managers coming together to imagine crises that have never before occurred and that might befall the organization, and how the organization would deal with them.

But these are all obvious payoffs of crisis preparedness. In order to really understand the on-the-ground difference between life in a crisis-prone versus a crisis-prepared environment, consider these two accounts. The first involves the burnout experienced by Canadian public service executives after attempting to manage crisis after crisis spawned from the COVID-19 pandemic.[2] Canada's Association of Professional Executives of the Public Service (APEX) reported in 2022 that their members were so burned out after working through the COVID-19 pandemic, many were calling and asking for advice on how to obtain voluntary demotions. Such requests were quite rare before the pandemic and caused significant concern for Canadian public service organizations; as APEX pointed out, this exodus had the potential to damage leadership quality as well the ability to attract new executive talent to public service organizations in the future.

These executives were in public organizations—people who have very likely spent years working their way up the ladder to those positions. After slogging through all the crises associated with the COVID-19 pandemic for two years, the executives were apparently so burned out that they were asking for demotions and were ready to walk away from the positions they had worked so hard to attain. This is a pretty good indication that their organizational contexts may be offering them little in terms of crisis preparation or support, as crisis procedures should, at the very least, be in place at this point.

Contrast the experience of these executives with this account of an executive at a community organization who, working with his team of board members and staff, weathered crisis after crisis, from an earthquake to wildfires to the protracted COVID-19 pandemic.[3] According to the account, on his very first day on the job in 2014 as president and CEO of the Napa Chamber of Commerce, Travis Stanley was welcomed by an earthquake. By bringing the community together quickly, surveying the damage, and listening to his constituents, Stanley was able to create a culture of support, aid, and preparation that facilitated collaboration across the different businesses he serves. This framework not only withstood several additional crises, but it also helped the community thrive for eight years during his tenure as CEO.

One might suggest this is an apples-to-oranges comparison, but consider that all the executives were in public service and managing the difficult period of time associated with the COVID-19 pandemic. Some were so emotionally spent, they were willing to walk away from their top-tier jobs and take lower-ranked, lower-paying jobs due to self-reported burnout. But one executive came through the other side with a more close-knit team and community to show for the experience. Yes, being in Napa Valley surrounded by vineyards might have helped—but so did building relationships and preparation mechanisms together.

As we have discussed, in addition to benefiting from visible top-level support, being a crisis-prepared organization entails having procedures and resources in place and, through training, possessing adaptive coordination and communication capabilities when a crisis emerges. How else might being a crisis-prepared organization be beneficial? First, it seems clear that being more prepared for crises increases the likelihood of achieving a better organizational outcome. A crisis-prepared organization is likely to notice and react to a crisis more swiftly, adapt procedures more accurately (or jettison obsolete ones), and enact decisions with coordinated precision as compared to other organizations. While no organization or team will have perfect information to base decisions upon during a crisis, being prepared likely enables more accurate, less biased processing of the information at hand.

Second, think about the different experiences of the executives we just described. Crisis preparation leads to a host of beneficial *individual-level* outcomes in our crisis-imbued world. People working in crisis-prepared organizations likely experience less stress at work than people in crisis-prone organizations, as they experience fewer crises overall and are more competent to deal with the crises they do encounter. Furthermore, they are likely to take less stress home with them to their families, and probably are able to sleep better and recover more quickly after each day or work shift, enhancing their cognitive and decision-making skills as compared to their stressed counterparts. This lower experienced stress also is less likely to lead to burnout and the decision to leave, resulting in the high level of "revolving door" turnover that we so often see in crisis-prone organizations. Finally, because individuals and their teams in crisis-prepared organizations are indeed trained and competent, they are likely to benefit psychologically from *feeling* more competent and resilient, which may positively influence other areas of their lives.

Similarly, getting through the crisis in good shape is not the only way organizations benefit from being crisis-prepared; other *organization-level* benefits exist as well. Crisis-prepared organizations are less likely to pay the price of the "revolving door" of stress-related turnover through constant employee searches and onboarding efforts. Absent the constant churn of turnover, the organization's culture can become more stable and supportive of strategic efforts, with better employee longevity, commitment, and buy-in. The knowledge embodied by seasoned employees will stop constantly leaving the organization in the form of burned-out employees, and instead will stay and contribute to organizational learning.

Finally, there are clear benefits at the *community and stakeholder level* that can be derived from organizations being crisis-prepared. If these organizations weather the storm of crises better than others, they may be likely to have less job loss, economically benefiting the communities surrounding them (think about support for things like schools, shops, religious institutions, and shared facilities via taxes). In addition to less economic stress, less job loss also means less *social* stress on a community, as there is less economic strain that could be translated into a source of domestic or family stress, and social support networks can remain stable. Other stakeholders that partner with a crisis-prepared organization may benefit from the association with an organization that managed a crisis well in numerous ways, including economic outcomes and positive reputation.

But despite the direct and spillover benefits of crisis preparation, list after list and survey after survey indicate that organizations remain woefully crisis-underprepared.[4] The collective COVID-19 experience may change this slightly, but we are not optimistic. In fact, we have come to believe that allowing an organization to remain crisis-prone is not only unwise; it is *unethical*.

THE ETHICS OF BEING PREPARED

Throughout the many years we have conducted research with teams like airline flight crews, nuclear power plant control room crews, trauma teams, and underground mine rescue teams, we have been surrounded by people in organizations and cultures where being prepared is a way of life. The cost of being unprepared, in terms of damage to lives and communities, is just too great, even unfathomable, to imagine. In these high-reliability organizations, error-free operations is the goal, and much has been written and discussed about finding the best way to approach achieving such an outcome.

In many such organizations, automated systems provide checks and re-dundancy for complex critical operations; in fact, many people ask whether or not human actors should be eliminated from processes wherever possible, in order to reduce variance and risk. But here is the problem: Unexpected, unimaginable crises still occur that require human decision-makers to take control, adapt, and act. Consider, for example, the "Miracle on the Hudson" landing of U.S. Airways Flight 1549 on January 15, 2009. Most of us know the story of Captain Chesley "Sully" Sullenberger and First Officer Jeffrey Skiles managing to land a crippled Airbus A320 on the Hudson River, saving all 155 people on board after a bird strike resulted in loss of all engine power. It should have been a boring, routine flight, handled largely by automated rou-tines and checklists. Until it *wasn't*. As Sully later remarked, "Everything is unprecedented until it happens for the first time."

Captain Sullenberger has credited his extensive training—including in Crew Resource Management (CRM), a holistic approach to crew-level safety involving communication and coordination—for enabling his crew to manage the events on the Hudson that day. Sullenberger and Skiles worked for a crisis-prepared organization. Had they prepared for *exactly* the crisis they faced—flying an A320, facing a total loss of power, and landing on the Hudson River? Of course not. But their extensive training prepared them with communication, coordination, and technical skills that transferred to that unique situation, and lives onboard and on the ground were saved because of that crisis preparation.

Consider a different type of organization with a different type of crisis, but with a similar amount of crisis preparation. In 2008, Maple Leaf Foods, a Canadian food processing giant, was responsible for a listeria outbreak emanating from its Toronto processing plant that ultimately took the lives of twenty customers who consumed tainted products, and sickened thousands more. The organization had training, procedures, and strong cultural values in place to address the crisis, quickly closing and decontaminating the plant. CEO Michael McCain acted immediately to take accountability and publicly apologize for the incident—an act later described by many as authentic crisis leadership.[5] The company's response to the crisis was regarded as exemplary, and today's training and orientation video material for new employees includes images of a hearse and keeps the crisis memory alive in the culture and consciousness of all organization participants, with a goal of setting the highest possible industry standards for food safety.

In these two examples—U.S. Airways and Maple Leaf Foods—the organizations did their best to avoid well-known, obvious crises and train people to be appropriately crisis-prepared. They took steps to train and be ready for those unknown situations that could occur at any moment. U.S. Airways did this through CRM and recurrent training for its pilots, as well as other crisis-related training throughout the organization. Maple Leaf Foods accomplished food safety–oriented training throughout the organization and also inculcated the organization with a strong safety- and community-centered culture. Both organizations were decidedly not the crisis mills that crisis-prone organizations become.

Now contrast life in these organizations with life in a crisis-prone organization. Allowing an organization to exist as crisis-prone exposes employees to unpredictable chains of crises events over time, given that the crisis-prone organization has inadequate capability to sense crises early on and avoid or truncate them (see Chapter 1). What does that do to people in these organizations? Remember that the "logic" of crisis-prone organizations is typically to hire really good, smart people who will somehow magically be able to "deal" with crises when they come up, and without any crisis preparation training, since the crisis-prone organization doesn't do preparation. These people, who are used to feeling pretty competent about their abilities, are faced with crisis after crisis, without the benefit of crisis preparation. Over time, compared to people in a crisis-prepared organization, these individuals are probably more likely to experience stress, burnout, feelings of low efficacy, helplessness, and, if they really care about the people they're serving and the job they do, even hopelessness. Taken together, these types of feelings can lead to social pain, psychological distress, and an overwhelming sense of defeat or entrapment. That's enough to lead many workers to snap, leaving their jobs suddenly and spontaneously—a phenomenon now referred to as "rage quitting."[6] Add to these negative outcomes something called "moral harm" if the critical situations encountered tend to be ethical in nature, placing people in the position of violating or being expected to violate their own values. The concept of "moral injury" is expertly described by Jori Pascal Kalkman and Tine Molendijk:[7]

"Moral injury" refers to the psychological suffering that may be engendered by performing, failing to prevent, or falling victim to actions that conflict with one's moral beliefs and expectations. This moral distress entails feelings of guilt, shame, or, conversely, a sense of betrayal and anger (Frankfurt & Frazier, 2016; Litz et al., 2009). More specific symptoms related to moral injury include a sense of meaninglessness, distrust towards others or oneself, and self- or other-punishing behaviors (Frankfurt & Frazier, 2016; Litz et al., 2009).

And the concept of moral injury may be even more prevalent when you realize that more CEOs are fired due to ethical transgressions than for poor financial performance,[8] *and* when you think about the plethora of ethical scandals in organizations today. Consider Ernst & Young's 2022 $100 million fine from the SEC, levied for hundreds of employees cheating on their ethics tests![9]

"So why don't these people just leave?" you might ask. People at lower levels of the organization with fewer skills may feel trapped and unable to find jobs elsewhere, as might people with very specific skills.[10] The result is that people churn through crisis after crisis, feeling helpless and burned out. The horrible combination of social and psychological pain, defeat, entrapment, and moral harm could even lead people to consider suicide. It may be more than coincidence that the increasing number of crises experienced by organizations mirrors the increasing suicide rate. As one group of researchers notes, suicide is the tenth leading cause of death in the United States, and the National Institute of Mental Health maintains that a comprehensive approach involving multiple stakeholders—including *employers*—is absolutely necessary to reduce the number of suicide deaths in the country.[11] Other researchers note that "each suicide, on average, impacts 135 people who personally knew the deceased, resulting in estimates of almost 6 million people affected by the suicide of another person each year."[12] And if all the pain and harm produced by the "crisis mill" in crisis-prone organizations does not result in an employee leaving the organization, severe burnout, or turning the pain inward, it seems plausible that the pain could be directed outward and become aggression and violence toward co-workers or supervisors perceived as abusive or unjust.[13]

Taken together, these are the reasons we believe that allowing an organization to remain crisis-prone is simply an unethical choice. *There is no excuse.*

It is difficult and takes a significant investment of time and other resources to create a crisis-preparation strategy and to engage in the anticipatory actions necessary to create and maintain a crisis-prepared organization. And that is exactly what ethical organizations owe their participants, stakeholders, and communities. In fact, this is congruent with the United Nations' conceptualization of social sustainability:

"Social sustainability is about identifying and managing business impacts, both positive and negative, on people. The quality of a company's relationships and engagement with its stakeholders is critical. Directly or indirectly, companies affect what happens to employees, workers in the value chain, customers and local communities, and it is important to manage impacts proactively."[14]

Indeed, crisis preparation is social sustainability. As emphasized by Dean Beth Walker at Colorado State University, whose award-winning strategic vision "Business for a Better World" enacts social sustainability tenets, preparation activities also have the benefit of involving people from every level of the organization in a sustainable activity, increasing their voice, involvement,

empowerment, commitment, and, perhaps most importantly, sense of compe-
tence and control.[15] To us, this sounds very much like an antidote to the social
and psychological pain, entrapment, and defeat of the crisis mill.

And finally, for those who cling to the view that corporations exist solely
to maximize shareholder wealth, and that any other undertaking (like treating people humanely via crisis preparation) is poppycock and grounds for a
shareholder lawsuit, just try maximizing shareholder wealth with a revolving
door of 40+ percent turnover and a mountain of wrongful death litigations,
not to mention a cascade of badly managed crises described in real-time all
over every type of social media. Good luck with that these days.

CONCLUSION

We hope the above argument is one that will prove useful for those seeking
to motivate decision-makers in organizations to shift their thinking and leadership to a more crisis-prepared stance. If you are an organizational decision-
maker, we hope to have either offered support for your crisis-preparation
activities or to have nudged your thinking and actions in that direction.

As we pointed out at the beginning of this book, more and more complex
crises are on the horizon for every organization. Why? Consider the turbu-
lence represented today in the factors identified in the classic strategic analysis
tool, the PESTEL framework.[16] The "PESTEL" mnemonic represents Political, Economic, Social, Technological, Environmental, and Legal forces across
different geographic areas. First, the *political* stability of many countries has
decreased, with democracies that have been stable for decades or centuries being threatened by authoritarian-leaning populist movements. The global *economic* situation has certainly become unstable in our post-COVID world as
organizations still struggle with supply chain, inflation, manufacturing, and
raw material issues. *Social* stability, many would argue, has deteriorated, fu-
eled by wealth distribution inequities, social justice tensions, and social value
polarization. *Technological* stability has also decreased, with countries poised
to create East vs. West factions in access and standards. And the situation with
our *environment* is anything but stable, although many individuals, organizations, and countries are acting to do what they can to slow the progression of
climate change. Finally, the *legal* environment across many countries seems

also in flux, influencing change in other PESTEL categories; witness, for example, the recent U.S. Supreme Court ruling that overturned *Roe v. Wade* and abortion access, or the announcement that Scotland will soon again hold a vote for independence from the United Kingdom.

Take all these PESTEL factors, throw them in a mixing bowl, add a heaping portion of unpredictable human nature, and what comes out? Crises that have never before been imagined. And in order to deal with them effectively, organizations will turn to *teams* of people—not single individuals—to deal with these monsters, again and again. We have done our best here to share what we have learned about teams facing crises—to help you, your teams, your organization, or your students prepare for handling critical situations. We truly believe that with more preparation and understanding of team behaviors during crises, not only will team and organization outcomes improve, but we will also see less stress carried home and ultimately healthier outcomes for the families and communities that sustain us.

NOTES

CHAPTER 1

1. National Transportation Safety Board. (2019, November 19). NTSB/AAR-19/03.

2. McCartney, S. (2018, April 24). At Southwest airlines, the minutes after disaster struck. *The Wall Street Journal.* https://www.wsj.com/articles/at-southwest-airlines-the-minutes-after -disaster-struck-1524586032

3. Campbell, J. (2012). *The hero with a thousand faces* (3rd ed.). New World Library.

4. Pearson, C. M., & Clair, J. A. (1998). Reframing Crisis Management. *Academy of Management Review, 23*(1), 59–76. https://doi.org/10.2307/259099

5. Clifford, S. (2009, April 15). Video prank at Domino's taints brand. *New York Times.* https:// www.nytimes.com/2009/04/16/business/media/16dominos.html

6. Coutu, D. (2003, April). Sense and reliability. *Harvard Business Review.* https://hbr.org/2003/04/ sense-and-reliability

7. Waller, M. J., & Uitdewilligen, S. (2008). Talking to the room: Collective sensemaking during crisis situations. In R. A. Roe, M. J. Waller, & S. Clegg (Eds.), *Time in organizational research* (pp. 208–25). Routledge.

8. Lerbinger, O. (2012). *The crisis manager: Facing disasters, conflicts, and failures* (2nd ed.). Routledge.

9. Waller, M. J., & Uitdewilligen, S. (2012). Transitions in action teams. In G. Graen & J. Graen (Eds.), *Management of teams in extreme context* (pp. 167–95). Information Age Publishing.

10. Magnusson, M. S. (2000). Discovering hidden time patterns in behavior: T-patterns and their detection. *Behavior Research Methods, Instruments, & Computers, 32*(1), 93–110. https://doi .org/10.3758/BF03200792

11. National Institutes of Health. (2023, January 26). *Enhancing reproducibility through rigor and transparency.* https://grants.nih.gov/policy/reproducibility/index.htm#

CHAPTER 2

1. Fong, K. (2020, February 29). 50 years on—how Apollo 13's near disastrous mission is relevant today. *The Guardian*. https://www.theguardian.com/science/2020/feb/29/apollo-13-how-teamwork -and-tenacity-turned-disaster-into-triumph

2. Zellmer-Bruhn, M., Waller, M. J., & Ancona., D. G. (2004). The effect of temporal entrainment on the ability of teams to change their routines. In S. Blount (Ed.), *Research on managing groups and teams* (vol. 6, pp. 236–66).

3. Waller, M. J., & Uitdewilligen, S. (2008). Talking to the room: Collective sensemaking during crisis situations. In R. A. Roe, M. J. Waller, & S. Clegg (Eds.), *Time in organizational research* (pp. 208–25). Routledge.

4. Rogelberg, S. G. (2018). *The surprising science of meetings: How you can lead your team to peak performance*. Oxford University Press.

5. Hoogeboom, M. A. M. G., & Wilderom, C. P. M. (2020). A complex adaptive systems approach to real-life team interaction patterns, task context, information sharing, and effectiveness. *Group & Organization Management, 45*(1), 3–42. https://doi.org/10.1177/1059601119854927

6. Wright, R., Butler, C., & Tarrant, S. (1999, January 8). Interview with Eugene F. Kranz. Johnson Space Center Oral History Project.

CHAPTER 3

1. Su, L., Kaplan, S., Burd, R., Winslow, C., Hargrove, A., & Waller, M. J. (2017). Trauma resuscitation: Can team behaviours in the prearrival period predict resuscitation performance? *British Medical Journal: Simulation & Technology Enhanced Learning, 3*(3), 106–110. doi.org/10.1136/ bmjstel-2016-000143

2. Zijlstra, F., Waller, M. J., & Phillips, S. (2012). Setting the tone: Early interaction patterns in swift starting teams as a predictor of effectiveness. *European Journal of Work and Organizational Psychology, 21*(5), 749–77. doi.org/10.1080/1359432X.2012.690399

CHAPTER 4

1. Uitdewilligen, S., & Waller, M. J. (2018). Information sharing and decision making in multidisciplinary crisis management teams. *Journal of Organizational Behavior, 39*(6), 731–48. doi.org/10.1002/job.2301

2. Mohammed, S., Ferzandi, L., & Hamilton, K. (2010). Metaphor no more: A 15-year review of the team mental model construct. *Journal of Management, 36*(4), 876–910. doi.org/10.1177/0149206309356804

3. De Dreu, C. K. W. (2007). Cooperative outcome interdependence, task reflexivity, and team effectiveness: A motivated information processing perspective. *Journal of Applied Psychology, 92*(3), 628–38. doi.org/10.1037/0021-9010.92.3.628

4. Sohrab, S., Uitdewilligen, S., & Waller, M. (2021). The temporal phase structure of team interaction under asymmetric information: The solution fixation trap. *Journal of Organizational Behavior, 43*(5), 892–911. doi.org/10.1002/job.2592

CHAPTER 5

1. Dowd, A. (2022, December 15). *Why Ukraine's "MacGyver" military is winning*. American Legion. https://www.legion.org/landingzone/257706/why-ukraine%E2%80%99s-%E2%80%98macgyver%E2%80%99 -military-winning

2. Bertrand, N., & Graef, A. (2023, March 22). *Ukrainian troops impress US trainers as they rapidly get up to speed on Patriot missile system*. CNN. https://www.cnn.com/2023/03/21/politics/ ukraine-troops-training-patriot-missile-system/index.html

3. Axe, D. (2023, March 25). The Ukrainian army needs more heavy vehicles. Until it gets them, creative tactics must suffice. *Forbes*. https://www.forbes.com/sites/davidaxe/2023/03/25/the-ukrainian -army-needs-more-heavy-vehicles-until-it-gets-them-creative-tactics-must-suffice/?sh=40ecc1cd7958

4. Tucker, A. L., & Edmondson, A. C. (2003). Why hospitals don't learn from failures: Organizational and psychological dynamics that inhibit system change. *California Management Review, 45*(2), 55–72. doi.org/10.2307/41166165

5. Staw, B. M., Sandelands, L. E., & Dutton, J. E. (1981). Threat rigidity effects in organizational behavior: A multilevel analysis. *Administrative Science Quarterly, 26*(3), 501–524. doi.org/10.2307/2392337

6. Bell, M., Facci, E., & Nayeem, R. (2005). Cognitive tunneling, aircraft-pilot coupling design issues and scenario interpretation under stress in recent airline accidents. *2005 International Symposium on Aviation Psychology*, 45–49. https://corescholar.libraries.wright.edu/isap_2005/7/

7. Weick, K. E. (1993). The collapse of sensemaking in organizations: The Mann Gulch disaster. *Administrative Science Quarterly, 38*(4), 628–52. doi.org/10.2307/2393339

8. Waller, M. J., & Uitdewilligen, S. (2012). Transitions in action teams. In G. Graen & J. Graen (Eds.), *Management of teams in extreme context* (pp. 167–95). Information Age Publishing.

CHAPTER 6

1. Waller, M. J. (1999). The timing of adaptive group responses to nonroutine events. *Academy of Management Journal, 42*(2), 127–37. doi.org/10.2307/257088

2. Allison, P. D. (1994). Using panel data to estimate the effects of events. *Sociological Methods & Research, 23*(2), 174–99. doi.org/10.1177/0049124194023002002

3. Waller, M. J., Gupta, N., & Giambatista, R. C. (2004). Effects of adaptive behaviors and shared mental models on control crew performance. *Management Science, 50*(11), 1534–44. doi.org/10.1287/mnsc.1040.0210

4. We've been told that the word "tailboard" originates from the U.S. Navy, and since most of the nuclear operators in the crews had spent time on U.S. Navy vessels, this makes sense to us.

5. Even though we labeled some of the crews "lower" performers for the purposes of our study, it's important to note that the performance of these crews was well above the minimum performance standards of the plant and of the national accrediting and licensing organizations.

CHAPTER 7

1. Waller, M. J., & Uitdewilligen, S. (2008). Talking to the room: Collective sensemaking during crisis situations. In R. A. Roe, M. J. Waller, & S. Clegg (Eds.), *Time in organizational research* (pp. 208–25). Routledge.

2. Bronner, M. (2006, September). 9/11 live: The NORAD tapes. *Vanity Fair*, 262–95. https:// archive.vanityfair.com/article/2006/9/911-live-the-norad-tapes

3. National Commission on Terrorist Attacks (2004). *The 9/11 commission report.* Norton.

4. Waller, M., Salvador, R., & Sutcliffe, K. (2024, January 23). Adaptation to discontinuous nonroutine events: Dual threats and the mediator of fear. In M. Griffin & G. Grote (Eds.), *The Oxford Handbook of Uncertainty Management in Work Organizations.* Oxford Academic. doi.org/10.1093/oxfordhb/9780197501061.013.21

CHAPTER 8

1. Adapted from Reason, J. (2008). *The human contribution: Unsafe acts, accidents, and heroic recoveries.* Ashgate Publishing, Ltd.

2. Note that here, we refer to the ability to appropriately balance a team's use of routines and improvisation *over time* during a crisis event. Earlier, when we discussed Adapting on the Fly (Chapter 5), we focused only on the ability of teams to detach from well-learned routines and realize when those approaches have become wholesale obsolete and no longer fit a crisis situation. These are two somewhat similar but distinctly different team skills.

3. Staw, B. M., Sandelands, L. E., & Dutton, J. E. (1981). Threat rigidity effects in organizational behavior: A multilevel analysis. *Administrative Science Quarterly, 26*(3), 501–524. doi.org/10.2307/2392337

4. Marks, M. A., Mathieu, J. E., & Zaccaro, S. J. (2001). A temporally based framework and taxonomy of team processes. *Academy of Management Review, 26*(3), 356–76. doi.org/10.2307/259182

5. While our focus is on verbal, in-person communication, much of this also holds for teams communicating electronically.

CHAPTER 9

1. Johnson, C. K., Gutzwiller, R. S., Gervais, J., and Ferguson-Walter, K. J. (2021). Decision-making biases and cyber attackers. *2021 36th IEEE/ACM International Conference on Automated Software Engineering Workshops (ASEW)*, Melbourne, Australia, 140–44. doi.org/10.1109/ASEW52652.2021.00038

2. Stachowski, A. A., Kaplan, S. A., & Waller, M. J. (2009). The Benefits of Flexible Team Interaction During Crises. *Journal of Applied Psychology, 94*(6), 1536–43. doi.org/10.1037/a0016903

3. Entin, E. E., & Serfaty, D. (1999). Adaptive team coordination. *Human Factors, 41*(2), 312–25. doi.org/10.1518/001872099779591196

CHAPTER 10

1. Lei, Z., Waller, M. J., Hagen, J., & Kaplan, S. (2016). Team adaptiveness in dynamic contexts: Contextualizing the roles of interaction patterns and in-process planning. *Group & Organization Management, 41*(4), 491–525. doi.org/10.1177/1059601115615246

CHAPTER 11

1. Waller, M., Kaplan, S., Torres, E., & Shulman, M. (2020). *When slower talk makes faster teams: Coordination and interaction in mine rescue teams* [Paper presentation]. Interdisciplinary Network for Group Research (INGRoup) Annual Meeting, Bellevue, WA.

2. NNL Staff. (2015, June 3). Top mine rescue competition in Thunder Bay. *Net News Ledger*. https://www.netnewsledger.com/2015/06/03/top-mine-rescue-competition-in-thunder-bay/

CHAPTER 12

1. Stevens, M. J., & Campion, M. A. (1994). The knowledge, skill, and ability requirements for teamwork: Implications for human resource management. *Journal of Management, 20*(2), 503–530. doi.org/10.1016/0149-2063(94)90025-6

2. Landy, F. J., Rastegary, H., Thayer, J., & Colvin, C. (1991). Time urgency: The construct and its measurement. *Journal of Applied Psychology, 76*(5), 644–57. doi.org/10.1037/0021-9010.76.5.644

3. Waller, M. J., Conte, J. M., Gibson, C. B., & Carpenter, M. A. (2001). The effect of individual perceptions of deadlines on team performance. *Academy of Management Review, 26*(4), 586–600. doi.org/10.2307/3560243

4. Zimbardo, P. G., & Boyd, J. N. (1991). Putting time in perspective: A valid, reliable individual-differences metric. *Journal of Personality and Social Psychology, 77*(6), 1271–88. doi.org/10.1037/0022-3514.77.6.1271

5. Ibid.

6. Waller, M. J., Franklin, A. E., & Parcher, D. B. (2020). Time perspective balance and team adaptation in dynamic task contexts. *Journal of Organizational Behavior, 41*(2), 263–75. doi.org/10.1002/job.2431

7. König, C. J., & Waller, M. J. (2010). Time for reflection: A critical examination of polychronicity. *Human Performance, 23*(2), 173–90. doi.org/10.1080/08959281003621703

8. Kaplan, S. A. (2008). Polychronicity in work teams: A theoretical examination of antecedents and consequences. In R. A. Roe, M. J. Waller, & S. Clegg (Eds.), *Time in organizational research* (pp. 103–126). Routledge.

9. Waller, M. J., Giambatista, R. C., & Zellmer-Bruhn, M. E. (1999). The effects of individual time urgency on group polychronicity. *Journal of Managerial Psychology, 14*(3), 244–56. doi.org/10.1108/02683949910263765

10. Kaplan, S. A., LaPort, K., & Waller, M. J. (2013). The role of positive affect in team performance during crises. *Journal of Organizational Behavior, 34*(4), 473–91. doi.org/10.1002/job.1817

11. Parker, S. H., Lei, X., Fitzgibbons, S., Metzger, T., Safford, S., & Kaplan, S. (2020). The impact of surgical team familiarity on length of procedure and length of stay: Inconsistent relationships across procedures, team members, and sites. *World Journal of Surgery, 44*(11), 3658–67. doi.org/10.1007/s00268-020-05657-1

CHAPTER 13

1. Udemy Business. *2022 learning trends: The power of soft skills.* https://business.udemy.com/resources/2022-learning-trends-power-soft-skills/

2. Freifeld, L. (Ed.) (2021, November 19). 2021 training industry report. *Training Magazine.* https://trainingmag.com/2021-training-industry-report/

3. Udemy Business. *2022 learning trends: The power of soft skills.* https://business.udemy.com/resources/2022-learning-trends-power-soft-skills/

4. McGaghie, W. C., Issenberg, S. B., Petrusa, E. R., & Scalese, R. J. (2010). A critical review of simulation-based medical education research: 2003–2009. *Medical Education, 44*(1), 50–63. doi.org/10.1111/j.1365-2923.2009.03547.x

5. Waller, M. J., Lei, Z., & Pratten, R. (2014). Focusing on teams in crisis management education: An integration and simulation-based approach. *Academy of Management Learning & Education, 13*(2), 208–221. doi.org/10.5465/amle.2012.0337

6. Ibid.

7. Waller, M. J., Lei, Z., & Pratten, R. (2014). Focusing on teams in crisis management education: An integration and simulation-based approach. *Academy of Management Learning & Education, 13*(2), 208–221. doi.org/10.5465/amle.2012.0337

8. Sarpy, S. A., Warren, C. R., Kaplan, S. A., Bradley, J. B., & Howe, R. (2005). Simulating public health response to a Severe Acute Respiratory Syndrome (SARS) event: A comprehensive systematic approach to designing, implementing, and evaluating a tabletop exercise. *Journal of Public Health Management and Practice,* S75–82. doi.org/10.1097/00124784-200511001-00013

9. Mathieu, J. E., Luciano, M. M., D'Innocenzo, L., Klock, E. A., & LePine, J. A. (2019). The development and construct validity of a team processes survey measure. *Organizational Research Methods, 23*(3), 399–431. doi.org/10.1177/1094428119840801. Salas, E., Reyes, D. L., & Woods, A. L. (2017). The assessment of team performance: observations and needs in innovative assessment of collaboration. In B. Veldkamp & M. von Davier (Eds.), *Methodology of educational measurement and assessment* (pp. 21–36). Springer: Switzerland.

10. Waller, M. J., & Kaplan, S. (2018). Systematic behavioral observation for emergent team phenomena: Key considerations for quantitative video-based approaches. *Organizational Research Methods, 21*(2), 500–515. doi.org/10.1177/1094428116647785

11. Issenberg, S., McGaghie, W. C., Petrusa, E. R., Gordon, D. L., & Scalese, R. J. (2005). Features and uses of high-fidelity medical simulations that lead to effective learning: A BEME systematic review. *Medical Teacher, 27*(1), 10–28. doi.org/10.1080/01421590500046924

12. Keiser, N. L., & Arthur, W. (2021). A meta-analysis of the effectiveness of the after-action review (or debrief) and factors that influence its effectiveness. *Journal of Applied Psychology, 106*(7), 1007–1032. doi.org/10.1037/apl0000821

13. Villado, A. J., & Arthur, W. (2013). The comparative effect of subjective and objective after-action reviews on team performance on a complex task. *Journal of Applied Psychology, 98*(3), 514–28. doi.org/10.1037/a0031510

14. Rudolph, J. W., Simon, R., Dufresne, R. L., & Raemer, D. B. (2006). There's no such thing as "nonjudgmental" debriefing: A theory and method for debriefing with good judgment. *Simulation in Healthcare: The Journal of the Society for Simulation in Healthcare, 1*(1), 49–55. https://journals.lww .com/simulationinhealthcare/fulltext/2006/00110/there_s_no_such_thing_as__nonjudgmental_.6.aspx

CHAPTER 14

1. Raetze, S., Duchek, S., Maynard, M. T., & Wohlgemuth, M. (2022). Resilience in organization-related research: An integrative conceptual review across disciplines and levels of analysis. *Journal of Applied Psychology, 107*(6), 867–97. doi.org/10.1037/apl0000952

2. Sutcliffe, K. M., & Vogus, T. J. (2003). Organizing for resilience. In K. Cameron, J. E. Dutton, & R. E. Quinn (Eds.), *Positive organizational scholarship: Foundations of a new discipline* (pp. 94–110). Berrett-Koehler.

3. Tucker, A. L., & Edmondson, A. C. (2003). Why hospitals don't learn from failures: Organizational and psychological dynamics that inhibit system change. *California Management Review, 45*(2), 55–72. doi.org/10.2307/41166165

4. Mitroff, I. I. (2003). *Crisis leadership: Planning for the unthinkable.* Wiley.

5. Frosch, D., & Carlton, J. (2023, August 12). Hawaii officials were warned years ago that Maui's Lahaina face high wildfire risk. *The Wall Street Journal.* https://www.wsj.com/articles/hawaii-maui -fire-risks-plans-government-e883f3a3

6. Fackler, M. (2011, June 1). Report finds Japan underestimated tsunami danger. *The New York Times.* https://www.nytimes.com/2011/06/02/world/asia/02japan.html

7. Larouzee, J., & Le Coze, J. C. (2020). Good and bad reasons: The Swiss cheese model and its critics. *Safety Science, 126,* 104660. doi.org/10.1016/j.ssci.2020.104660

8. Jefferson, A., Bortolotti, L., & Kuzmanovic, B. (2017). What is unrealistic optimism? *Consciousness and Cognition, 50,* 3–11. doi.org/10.1016/j.concog.2016.10.005

9. Pearson, C. M., & Mitroff, I. I. (1993). From crisis prone to crisis prepared: A framework for crisis management. *Academy of Management Executives, 7*(1), 48–59. https://www.jstor.org/stable/4165107

10. Cirka, C. C., & Corrigall, E. A. (2010). Expanding possibilities through metaphor: Breaking biases to improve crisis management. *Journal of Management Education, 34*(2), 303–323. doi.org/10.1177/1052562910380657

11. Mitroff, I. I., & Alpaslan, M. C. (2003, April). Preparing for evil. *Harvard Business Review.* https://hbr.org/2003/04/preparing-for-evil

12. Uitdewilligen, S., & Waller, M. J. (2012). Adaptation in multiteam systems: The role of temporal semistructures. In S. J. Zaccaro, M. A. Marks, & L. A. DeChurch (Eds.), *Multiteam systems: An organization form for dynamic and complex environments* (pp. 365–94). Routledge.

13. Kaplan, S. A., & Waller, M. J. (2018). Reliability through resilience in organizational teams. In R. Ramanujam & K. H. Roberts (Eds.), *Organizing for reliability: A guide for research and practice* (pp. 90–117). Stanford Business Books.

14. Klein, Gary A. (1993). A recognition-primed decision (RPD) model of rapid decision making. In G. A. Klein, J. Orasanu, R. Calderwood, & C. E. Zsambok (Eds.), *Decision making in action: Models and methods* (pp. 138–47). Ablex Publishing.

15. Leveson, N., Dulac, N., Marais, K., & Carroll, J. (2009). Moving beyond normal accidents and high reliability organizations: A systems approach to safety in complex systems. *Organization Studies, 30*(2–3), 227–49. doi.org/10.1177/0170840608101478

16. Ramanujam, R., & Roberts, K. H. (Eds.). (2018). *Organizing for reliability: A guide for research and practice.* Stanford Press.

CHAPTER 15

1. Levenson, M. (2020, March 23). Anheuser-Busch and distilleries race to make hand sanitizer amid coronavirus pandemic. *The New York Times.* https://www.nytimes.com/2020/03/19/us/distilleries -virus-hand-sanitizer.html

2. May, K. (2022, April 7). Some public service executives "burned out" by crisis management. *Policy Opinions.* https://policyoptions.irpp.org/magazines/april-2022/some-public-service-executives -burned-out-by-crisis-management/

3. Bunn, C. (2020, November 3). *A former NBA executive is leading Napa's businesses through crisis after crisis.* NBC News. https://www.nbcnews.com/news/nbcblk/former-nba-executive-leading -napa-s-businesses-through-crisis-after-n1245906

4. Andriole, S. (2021, January 19). Why crisis managers fail & why preparation is a myth. *Forbes.* https://www.forbes.com/sites/steveandriole/2021/01/19/why-crisis-management-never-happens-why -preparation-is-a-myth/?sh=33dd71b32180

5. Greenberg, J., & Elliott, C. (2009). A cold cut crisis: Listeriosis, Maple Leaf Foods, and the politics of apology. *Canadian Journal of Communication, 34*(2),189–204. doi.org/10.22230/cjc.2009v34n2a2204

6. Smith, B. (2022). Stemming the rising tide of anger in the workplace: How to build emotion control among employees before anger spills out. *Strategic HR Review, 21*(2), 50–53. doi.org/10.1108/SHR-01-2022-0001

7. Kalkman, J. P., & Molendijk, T. (2021). The role of strategic ambiguity in moral injury: A case study of Dutch Border guards facing moral challenges. *Journal of Management Inquiry, 30*(2), 221–34. doi.org/10.1177/1056492619892693

8. McGregor, J. (2019, May 15). More CEOs were forced out for ethical lapses in 2018 than poor financial performance. *The Washington Post.* https://www.washingtonpost.com/business/2019/05/15/more-ceos-were-forced-out-ethical-lapses-than-poor-financial-performance/#

9. Newmyer, T. (2022, June 28). Ernst & Young hit with $100 million fine over cheating on ethics tests. *The Washington Post.* https://www.washingtonpost.com/business/2022/06/28/ernst-young-cheating-sec-fine/

10. Crane M. F., Phillips, J. K., & Karin, E. (2017). "I've been a long time leaving": The role of limited skill transferability in increasing suicide-related cognitions and behavior in veterinarians. *Suicide and Life-threatening Behavior, 47*(3), 309–320. doi.org/10.1111/sltb.12279

11. Howard, M. C., Follmer, K. B., Smith, M. B., Tucker, R. P., & Van Zandt, E. C. (2022). Work and suicide: An interdisciplinary systematic literature review. *Journal of Organizational Behavior, 43*(2), 260–85. doi.org/10.1002/job.2519

12. Cerel, J., & Sanford, R. L. (2018). It's not who you know, it's how you think you know them: suicide exposure and suicide bereavement. *The Psychoanalytic Study of the Child, 71*(1), 76–96. pep-web.org/search/document/PSC.071.0076A

13. Barling, J., Dupré, K. E., & Kelloway, E. K. (2009). Predicting workplace aggression and violence. *Annual Review of Psychology, 60*(1), 671–92. doi.org/10.1146/annurev.psych.60.110707.163629

14. United Nations Global Compact. *Social sustainability.* Retrieved February 10, 2024, from https://www.unglobalcompact.org/what-is-gc/our-work/social

15. Personal conversation (2022, June 21).

16. Business to You. *Scanning the environment: PESTEL analysis.* Retrieved February 10, 2024, from https://www.business-to-you.com/scanning-the-environment-pestel-analysis/

INDEX

HIGH RELIABILITY AND CRISIS MANAGEMENT
Series Editors: Karlene H. Roberts and Rangaraj Ramanujam